CW01619963

3 STRIKES

The True Story of
Two Sisters that Survive
The Abuse of their Step Father

Kelly Sutherain

This is the work of nonfiction. The events and conversations in this book havc been set down to the best of the author's ability, although some names and details have been changed to protect the privacy of individuals.

First paperback edition December 2019

ISBN 978-1-9162881-0-2 (paperback)

ISBN 978-1-9162991-1-9 (eBook)

This book is dedicated to my sister, who had the courage and the strength to tell someone about what was happening to us. Through sheer strength and hope, she gave us the gift of love and joy.

This book is also dedicated to all the people involved, including:

Roger and Tanya
Sylvia Matthews
Gordon Matthews
Caroline Lyden
Graham Lyden
Jean Metcalfe
Maurice Metcalfe

To all of you, for your support and encouragement throughout the years and for showing me the way of life. Without you all I would not be here today.

AUTHOR'S NOTES

This book is based on a true story; my real-life story from the ages of five to sixteen. Parts of my story are told from the perspective of a child, portraying the use of language and feeling that I felt as a young child.

Some of the names in this book have been changed to maintain their privacy and dignity.

CHAPTER ONE

MY FIRST GOODBYES

MY STORY BEGINS in a room.

It was unfamiliar and not my own, the rusty metal double bed filling most of the tiny space. The heavy bedspread was a light cream colour, complete with extremely faint flower prints that seemed to have faded through the many washes and years of use.

As you entered you were greeted with plain cream wallpaper, which – if you looked closely enough – had started to peel at the bottom of the wall. These walls would often echo with laughter, with children playing or people shouting.

Outside of these four walls, there was a very busy place through which many people constantly came and went. I wasn't sure what place we were in exactly, but I knew people didn't stay there for very long. I also knew this was not my home.

At the end of the bed there was a bare open sink, fixed right up against the wall, all by itself. Like a wandering dog without a master, the sink looked rather odd and lonely. I remember thinking to myself: where was the bath and toilet? What was the sink there for?

I was five years old and sharing a double bed with my younger sister, who was three at the time. I didn't mind sharing, though I will admit it felt a little strange as back at home, my sister and I had our own beds.

We hadn't been in this strange place for very long when, one evening, Daddy entered this unfamiliar room, dressed from head to toe in white as bright as the driven snow. I was used to seeing Daddy dressed in white; he was a chef in the army and would often tell me stories about what he'd cooked that day for all the men.

To me, my daddy always looked like a guardian angel, dressed in his neatly pressed bright white uniform, with a white cap and shiny black boots that you could almost see your own reflection in. His smile, however, was the most angelic thing about him.

We lived in a town called Mendez in Germany, in army houses within the barracks. This small town housed all the mummies and daddies that worked in the army, and everyone knew each other – and, therefore, knew each other's business. All the children would play together and run down our very own private street, like ripples through water.

Amongst all the daddies mine seemed perfect. He was tall and weighed 190 pounds. His hair was bushy, thick, and dark, and would often peep over the sides of his white army cap.

But on this particular evening, Daddy did not greet us with smiles; instead he frowned with worry as, in one fell swoop, he picked both me and Sarah up from the bed. Then, resting one of us on each hip, he quickly proceeded to walk us out of the room and down the hall towards the large wooden door at the end, the door that led out of this huge house that was occupied by so many others.

He flung this door wide open, letting in the dark and the rush of cool air that rippled through my nighty, sharply pungent. I tried to ignore it; instead I concentrated on my daddy's face, shining above his gleaming white uniform.

I flashed him a questioning look, asking, "Daddy, where are we going?"

Without hesitation he replied, "Home," and with that I lay my head on his shoulders, before resting my heavy eyes.

Prior to that unfamiliar room, I don't remember much of my very early childhood, except that I was relatively happy. We were never short of anything, but nor were we spoilt. I don't remember wanting for anything, but I'm sure if we did, we were given it. I don't generally remember many material things at home, other than a large wooden dining table that was situated at the side of the living room, which I had to stand on my tiptoes to see over the top of. I also remember that Daddy was always surrounded by friends who came to visit; I remember he would often hold parties on summer days in the back garden, where he would take charge of the barbecue in order to show off his brilliant cooking skills.

Whenever they entertained, Mummy would be full of smiles around him – she would smile so softly she filled a room of silence with speech – but I could not say the same for when they were alone. Mummy would often look tired and concerned. When she smiled at him it looked false, her sigh heavy as she daintily patted her tears from her cheeks. I would often see glassy tears shift from the corner of her eyes, down her tender cheeks and would wonder why she was crying again.

Mummy was petite and much smaller than Daddy, with short brown mousy hair that would often curl up at the bottom if she didn't dry it fully. She was just so beautiful to me. I often drank in everything she did, eager to learn how she managed to keep Daddy smiling while also looking after me and Sarah. To touch her face it was smooth, and I would often watch in awe as she applied her makeup, turning herself into a flawless woman, always tucking a piece of her hair behind her ear as she worked. She looked too unreal.

Sarah had inherited Mummy's looks; she had curly brown mousy hair that seemed to fall perfectly down her back, with the odd curl that hung like a solitary stooge – unlike my hair, which was blonde, frail, and straight.

Our family seemed perfect, just Mummy, Daddy, Sarah and I – full of laughter when people were around but not so much when we were alone. I would often see Mummy pacing back and forth across the living room, like shadows through a gloaming land, whilst Sarah and I played on the floor. I never understood why she did this, or why, when Daddy appeared, the pacing would stop.

On days like this – when Daddy was home – Sarah and I would be sent to our room. I never understood what Daddy could have done to make Mummy so mad, but those days became more and more frequent. I could never hear directly what the shouting was about – just echoes, an unpleasing ache to my ears, taunted like the scratching of nails across a blackboard. But, as time went on, Mummy began to stop her pacing, and when Daddy returned from work, instead of shouting there would be a silence so full of tension you could cut the ice-cold air with a knife.

Then, one day, Mummy was pacing up and down the stairs, going back and forth as she carried clothes and placed them on the big brown wooden table. I decided to approach the table and tried to peer over the top. Mummy was standing to the right of me, folding the clothes into piles.

"Where are we going, Mummy?" I asked.

"Away," Mummy replied in a quick, sharp, anxious tone. I'd never heard Mummy speak to me this way before. It was new and worrying.

I must have fallen asleep as I knew nothing of what had happened, my tall, dark, handsome, white-uniformed Daddy that had whisked me and Sarah away, must have put us back in this room, this unfamiliar room with the sink.

I knew nothing of where Daddy had taken us. Did we even go home? I wondered. How and why did Daddy return us to this room? Did Daddy even say goodbye? I wiped my tired eyes, searching around this unfamiliar room that we'd returned to.

No, wait – was that my daddy? He had his back turned to me and was washing his hands at the sink. I could not quite work out who it was. It was definitely a man, just as tall as my daddy with dark hair, but this man's hair was thin and shorter, his body type was stockier, and he didn't wear a white uniform; instead he wore a pastel grey and brown uniform.

With one hand he reached to the side of the sink, where a pair of glasses lay. He grabbed them before raising his hand towards his face. My daddy didn't wear glasses, this I knew.

This man turned around to look us over, while carefully placing the glasses back on his nose. His dark hair framed his snowy complexion, his face as pale as a ghost – and he behaved accordingly.

I knew then that this was not my daddy.

He walked towards Mummy and turned to politely kiss her on the cheek. "I'll see you later," he said to her with a distinct American accent that sounded strange and unfamiliar. Not a word did he speak to welcome us. Who could this man be?

I carefully placed my eyes upon his uniform, which looked familiar – it seemed like many of the army uniforms I'd seen at home, worn by my friend's daddies.

Mummy introduced him to us. "Now girls, this is Greg, and he's going to be staying with us for a while."

Where was Daddy? Why were we not going home? And why were we living here?

I had so many questions, but as he peered down at me – his eyes piercing right through me, like an unwelcome flash of light that left an everlasting mark upon its victim – I didn't dare ask any.

Even though Mummy had told us both that Greg was going to stay with us for a while, it wasn't long before the familiar sight of Mummy pacing up and down with clothes in her hands returned. We had remained in this room for a couple of days now, and I'd seen neither Greg nor Daddy. Once again, an undefined sadness seemed to have fallen about her like a cloud. We were packing again. Were we going home?

Despite Mummy being sad, I was overjoyed that we were finally leaving this place – just Mummy, me, and Sarah.

"Daddy!" Sarah and I screamed when we saw Daddy's car pull up in front of us, dropping all that we possessed (in suitcases and black bags) like a sack of potatoes as we ran over. He was finally here to take us home.

Yet, Mummy had said nothing to us. Who was Greg and why had we stayed in that room for so long without Daddy? All these unanswered questions and unwanted thoughts lurked deep within me, but in that moment, they couldn't have been further from my mind. I was just so happy to be going home!

As Daddy and Mummy opened the boot of the car to put the bags in, we climbed into the back seat. Daddy explained that we were going on a big boat and that we were going back to England to see my nanny and grandad; we were going to live with them for a short while whilst Mummy sorted a few things out.

What did Mummy need to sort out? I wondered, but I didn't care much as in that moment we were all back together – all four of us.

It was dark, and in no time at all I could feel myself drifting off as I stared out the car window at the passing lights.

Sometime later I slowly awoke to the sounds of Daddy telling me and Sarah to wake up, letting us know we were there. I wasn't sure how long the journey had been, but I couldn't help but feel excited, especially when I saw where we were.

There, out of the corner of my eye, I saw this massive white boat. 'Wow' I said to myself as we got into a long line of cars awaiting to be directed onto the boat. I couldn't believe that cars were allowed on boats!

In no time at all, the boat used the loud blast of its horn to let us know it had docked. I must have fallen asleep again, because by now I could see the sun rising over the tops of the clouds.

The noise of the boat was loud; it pierced your eardrums if you stood too close, though I supposed they needed to let everybody know when it was going to depart. I couldn't wait to get to Nanny and Grandad's, even though I didn't remember them and had no idea what they looked like or what to expect.

When the boat arrived at its destination we got off and continued driving until we came at last to a cluster of very small fine-looking homes. Mummy explained that Nanny and Grandad lived in Aldershot and had been living there for several years.

As we approached the house, I got a closer look. It was strange-looking – small, and nothing like the house in Germany. Where was the upstairs?

Daddy turned the car to park on their drive, and they must have known we were arriving as they came out to greet us before we'd even parked.

Mummy was the first to get out of the car, and as she did so the older woman walked over to her, greeting her warmly. They hugged so tightly it looked as though it was long overdue.

Staring out the front of the car, I observed this older lady. She had short brown hair and wasn't much taller than Mummy herself, though she was definitely older than Mummy; she wore a map of wrinkles across her face. I was drawn to her warm smile and her bright eyes, bursting as though ready to tell an incredible tale. I explored her wrinkles, thinking they told a story about someone who had loved, lived, suffered, and grieved. I knew she was a part of me and of who I was.

When Daddy got out the car he was greeted by an older sophisticated gentleman – in a more formal way of shaking hands –both with smiles on their faces. This man was much taller and had a head full of thick white hair.

"Come on, girls, out of the car!" Mummy said. "This is Nanny and Grandad."

"Hello Kelly and Sarah," Nanny said, in the softest, most welcoming tone.

With that said, Grandad seized both me and Sarah, pulling us up into his arms. He then grabbed my nose, pretending he'd removed it with his hand, and headed towards the house.

Inside, the house was beautiful. It had a perfectly clutter-free kitchen – complete with modern-looking light grey and cream cupboards – and a side door that led onto the driveway. At one end of the kitchen there was a small, round dining table, with four chairs neatly tucked underneath. I imagined this to be a place of gathering for chats, whilst sipping on a hot cup of tea.

The living room was designed with floral wallpaper. Even though I didn't have much experience in entering an older person's house, I could tell that

Nanny must have loved flowers, for every room I visited had similar designs of flowers over the walls.

Nanny and Grandad had several antiques on show in the living room, ornaments that you could tell were precious with the way they'd been placed in the cabinets for all to see. However, the one thing that struck me the most was a big wooden clock attached to the wall, the kind with chimes that hung right down to the bottom. I noticed a little door at the top of the clock and asked what it was for.

"This is a wooden cuckoo clock," Grandad explained. "On the hour the bird will come out of the doors and chirp for you."

As I couldn't yet tell the time, I asked when it was going to be an hour, so I could be there to greet this bird.

"Soon," he replied, smiling, "soon."

Leading on from the living room there was a bathroom to the right, one bedroom to the left – which I was instructed was Nanny and Grandad's room – and a bedroom directly in front, which had a sliding door looking out on the most wonderful garden. Nanny had a swinging double chair outside – complete with comfy-looking padded cushions – and lots and lots of flower beds.

"Can I go outside?" I asked – not to see the flowers, of course, but to have a go on the fun swinging chair.

"Of course," Nanny replied, "but stay away from my flowers."

I chuckled to myself as I carefully opened the door that led out to the garden, running immediately over to the swinging chair. It was just as comfy as it looked, and just as fun too.

After what seemed like hours of swinging on the chair, I was called back into the house to say goodbye to Daddy. I didn't know where Daddy was going or why he was going; all I was told was that he had to return to Germany for work. He had an important job to do, feeding all the men that were in the army.

I didn't really mind, I suppose, as we had everything we needed here at Nanny and Grandad's – I even had what seemed like a big sister. Her name was Caroline and she was fifteen years old. She was Mummy's little sister, and my auntie.

It was cramped sometimes at night-time, as Auntie Caroline would share a bed with Mummy, while me and Sarah would top and tail in another, all in the same room. But no one complained.

Auntie Caroline was beautiful. I would often sit and look at her, thinking how I wanted to be just like her. She had thick, curly, mousy brown hair, reaching just below her shoulders, and she was always funny, making everyone around her laugh. She just seemed to really love life. She spent half the day in the bathroom – shampooing her hair and painting her nails – and I would perch myself on the hallway floor, waiting for her to emerge so I could watch her apply her makeup before she went out for the night.

In order to be like her, my sister and I would play with my favourite toy (and one of the only ones I'd managed to bring with me from Germany), the teacup set. But we didn't pretend to drink tea; we would carefully put our feet into the colourful plastic cups and start to walk around, pretending we had high heels on. I wanted so much to be like Auntie Caroline, all grown up and happy.

Weeks went by and Sarah and I quickly became accustomed to Nanny's house. We didn't attend school, so most of our time was either spent in the house or walking their dog, Lucky. Lucky, a Dalmatian, was a very well-behaved dog, and the responsibility of walking him was often left to Auntie Caroline. Me and Sarah would ache to go with Caroline, to run alongside Lucky, feeling the frosty breeze blow across our faces, brushing our feet in amongst the shrivelled Autumn leaves.

One of my most memorable times there – and one of the things I used to love doing at Nanny and Grandad's – was having a bath. Nanny had this soap that smelt so unique that I couldn't relate it to anything, other than the sweet fresh smell it left on

Nanny's skin. This soap intrigued me, as it had a piece of square paper right in the centre of it, always staying on, no matter how many times you tried to pick it off. Every time I picked this soap up to wash myself, I took a little piece of Nanny with me. I would never forget this smell, and somehow, I knew that the smell would linger with me always reminding me of Nanny.

On days I felt down I would sit on Grandad's knee; I missed the cuddles from Daddy, which led to me getting them from Grandad instead. Grandad never minded, but whenever he needed to get up, he would quickly snap my nose into his hand and ask me where my nose had gone. After a couple of times of Grandad doing this, I would laugh and say, "Here, silly!" as I touched my own nose.

Once more time had passed, and Mummy began to toss and turn in bed, as if she were uncomfortable. I had noticed that Mummy's slender figure had begun to widen but I didn't know the reason behind it. I'd also noticed that Mummy would often have to stop, if she was walking or doing any house chores for Nanny and pause for a moment. She was breathing rather strange, with a heavy kind of panting. It didn't occur to me to ask her about it, though I did wonder if she was sick.

I never really gave Daddy much of a thought at Nanny and Grandad's house, probably because I was so happy.

Then, one day, when I entered the living room from the back garden, this familiar-looking man was standing there, being greeted by Nanny and Grandad. Do I know this man? I asked myself as I approached. I recognised the tone of his voice – it was cold and uncaring – and I knew it wasn't Daddy. He had a familiar face that I'd seen once before...

It was Greg!

But why was Greg here at Nanny and Grandad's house? I struggled in the desire to comprehend what was going on, my eyes widening as I sat bewitched, trying not to suffocate in the discussion.

He was standing there with a suitcase and a smug, satisfied look on his face, as if he had just won a bet. His presence made me feel uneasy, and even Lucky didn't attempt to greet him like he usually did with visitors.

Sarah's eyes met mine, and we simply sat there with our shocked faces until Mummy gave us an appraising glance. Yet not all was lost – I still had Nanny, Grandad, and Auntie Caroline for comfort.

Greg ended up staying with us. Mummy and Greg would often leave the home together, disappearing, so when Mummy didn't return home for a few days, I thought nothing of it. I was happy in this bubble of mine and no one could take that away from me.

Then Mummy did return with Greg – and this time they weren't alone.

This was my second significant earliest memory; the arrival of my baby brother, George. Mummy had left Sarah and me with Nanny and Grandad, and while I never fully understood what was going on, I knew one thing: Mummy had left without a baby and then had returned with one.

In came this pram with a tiny baby lying in it.

"This is your baby brother, George," Mummy had said to Sarah and me, smiling widely and oblivious to our confusion.

Where was George going to sleep? I wondered. Little did I know that we were soon to move out of Nanny and Grandad's house and into our own house with Greg.

So, within a few months I'd found myself having to say goodbye to my home in Germany, goodbye to Daddy, and now goodbye to Nanny and Grandad – and another home I'd come to love.

CHAPTER TWO

HIM

TOTLAND CLOSE IN Farnborough was a huge place. The flats had been designed in a square, with many shops directly beneath them; above the shops stood two floors of flats, and behind the first set of flats were another set of flats. At each corner of the square there were flights of stairs leading to two floors of flats above. A pathway ran directly through the centre of the square and right around the many shops. On the grassy square there lay a rickety old brown bench with a silver plaque – in memory of someone who perhaps used to live there, I thought. Perhaps it was an attempt from the local housing association to try and bring some life to the square, making it seem homely rather than the concrete jungle it actually was. The flats were surrounded by many people – anyone could walk into this complex from the outside, so you never knew who truly lived there or not – and this was to be our new home.

It was also to be a new start. What used to be a family of four, was now five.

When we arrived there, we set off tagging along behind Mummy, walking up the two flights of stairs to get to our flat.

Soon we were greeted by a striking blue door, one that led into our very own flat. We entered and Mummy proceeded to show us around.

This flat felt very different from our house back in Germany. Mummy and Greg's bedroom was the first room I saw, it being located directly in front of you as you came in the front door. I also noticed there was no garden – where would we have our barbecues when we invited friends and family over?

Walking upstairs, we were greeted by a further two more bedrooms on the right. The first room was smaller and was to be George's, while the next room – which was much larger – was to be mine and Sarah's. Directly in front of us, we were greeted by a dark, dreary room, the bathroom, which appeared to have no window. It was so dark that I couldn't work out the colour of this room; I could only just work out the white toilet that sat staring back at us as we peered in.

Past the bathroom and through the tiny hallway, we found the living room on the left, which then followed through to the very long, narrow kitchen. Between the living room and the bathroom was a door to the right, though I thought this to be unimportant as Mummy did not go on to mention or introduce this room at all.

The living room had a deep brown carpet, a couch in the centre of the room, and one single chair to the left of the couch, placed at an angle. Little did I know then that I would come to despise this brown carpet. To the left was an old worn brown cabinet that had a section for bottles, neatly stacked side by side. The cabinet was tall and wide and had a pull-down cupboard that was placed right in the centre of it. I knew these bottles were spirits and were not for touching, as back home in Germany Mummy and Daddy had a special section for their alcohol that Sarah and I were warned not to touch. Directly in front of the couch was a big window that showed you the back of our square, leading onto the next square behind that.

Apart from the front door, everything was dull and pale in the flat; there was no colour, unlike Nanny's home that was littered with colourful flower prints. Mummy and Greg must have already been there to prepare the flat, as all our things were already here, set out neatly.

I immediately ran to my room with excitement, so desperate to see the layout and what was waiting for me in there.

When I flung open the door, however, my excitement melted away. The floor – which consisted of a grey carpet with patches of different coloured stains – was bare and cold-looking. There was a big double bed that, once again I assumed, I would be sharing with Sarah. In the middle of this room was a small but tall wooden table, which stood on one leg. It looked to have no purpose, yet the solid wood had been carefully carved with such precision, it looked too invaluable to throw away. It also stuck out like a sore thumb, however, and I wasn't quite sure what to do with it. Looking further down the room, my eyes lit up when I saw my familiar toys that I had become accustomed to and loved to play with. There, in the middle of them, sat my teacups, which brought back wonderful memories of Auntie Caroline.

This is where I remember mine and Sarah's life becoming difficult. Rather than it being a memorable one for the right reasons, it became a living nightmare.

George was tiny – almost doll-like – and I had loved to play with him and give him cuddles at Nanny and Grandad's house, but I was soon forced to start comforting George instead, and not through love but through sheer fear. This began to feel like a chore in my daily routine, with no structure to it whatsoever – it was just random, whenever George decided to wake or needed the extra special attention.

George would cry like babies do and the words 'go see to your brother' were installed in me from Greg, which was when I started to look at Greg differently. There was no love when I looked at him, just fear. His face became meaner with each day that passed, going from being rather indifferent to the children he'd 'inherited' to as if he despised Sarah and me. He hardly ever looked at us, but when he did, I felt like it was with hatred – like we were a burden to be around.

It all started with George.

George had this pram that he was often put in and rocked to sleep. I remember that the carrycot part detached from the pram, and it was brown on the outside and cream on the inside.

One day George started to cry, and Greg ordered me to go and get him back off to sleep.

I had no idea how to do this, other than to sit next to him and rub his tummy. "George, I'm here, please don't cry," I would say to him, though it never did much. Hastily, I looked around for his dummy. 'Where is it?' I would murmur to myself. 'Oh, there it is, George – you were lying on it.' With that, George would stop crying and would stare up at me with his big blue eyes. I never knew how long I was supposed to sit there for, but I would stay a long while, until Mummy or Greg relieved me of my duty.

I was seven years old by this point and Sarah and I were to attend a new school. This school was called Mayfield Primary School and was just a short walk through the square. I was excited but frightened at the same time. What if nobody likes me? I wondered. Would I make any friends?

Directly next to our school was Mayfield Nursery, with a field separating the two schools.

When the first day of school arrived, Sarah and I got up to get ready. Mummy was already in the living room; where my bedroom was positioned, I could see directly ahead into that room. She was sitting in the chair, feeding George as he lay in her arms.

I wanted to make sure I wasn't late for school, so I quickly got dressed and asked Mummy what was for breakfast. I was used to helping myself, so when she told me to have cereal, I reached into the kitchen cupboards to grab the box, along with two bowls. I proceeded to pour the Rice Krispies into the bowls, the crackling sounds of this cereal intriguing me as always. I felt grown up, helping Mummy out while she was busy with George.

As I attempted to put the box of cereal back into the cupboard, however, the box slipped from my hands and fell to the floor. I hurriedly tried to pick this up and as I did, I felt a presence beside me, one that made my skin crawl.

I turned to see Greg standing there, the strangest expression on his face. I was frozen to the spot, and before I could even blink, he lifted his hand to deliver me a stinging, hard slap across my cheek. I clasped my cheek with my hand and before I could recover from the shock of what just happened, he lifted his other hand to scorn my other cheek with his presence. I could feel the blood as it drained from my already pale face, leaving only his red handprints from those strong, purposeful slaps.

I turned to look at Sarah, who seemed just as caught up in this nightmare as I was; her pale young face was blank, and she had a hollow look in her eyes that was cast over by a shadow.

My eyes began to swell. I didn't mean to drop the box – with all the excitement of wanting to help, I was just too quick for my own good.

Greg did not say a word. His stone-cold body walked away from me, leaving me to wonder why he'd smacked me across the face for simply dropping the box. It had been just one mistake, after all.

I fell to my knees to pick the box back up as

quickly as I could – conscious that he might come back – and as I gazed over at Mummy, I could see the look of sadness in her eyes, yet she said and did nothing. She'd been there the whole time, had seen everything. And yet she hadn't even moved.

I was no longer hungry – nor looking forward to school – as I tried to stop the tears from streaming down my face.

Arriving at school, I got to meet all the teachers and was directed around as the new pupil. It was exciting, but I could barely concentrate on anything, so worried was I about returning home. In fact, this soon became a regular occurrence.

Although I loved school, I loved it for all the wrong reasons. It was a place to go that was away from home, where all I had to do was worry about when it would be time to go home.

Every day at home was different; there was no routine other than having to attend school. I would often have to look after George when I returned home, doing the job of the parent. We were two children that spent our days tiptoeing around the place, trying to be quiet. We would also play in our bedroom, trying to find solace in what little toys we had.

With looking after my little brother, I was given this big responsibility that soon turned into a burden, as I feared getting into trouble. I would often panic, wondering what would happen if I couldn't settle him, or couldn't get him to sleep. Rather than concentrating on George, I would just sit there, pondering how long I would have to sit in the room before I could come out.

Then, one day, I was unable to settle George at all. He cried and cried, continuing to howl louder and louder. I wanted to pick George up, but my arms ached too much from pushing the carrycot back and forth.

After a while Greg approached me, ordering me to bring the carrycot upstairs and into the living room. It was far too heavy for my little arms, and I had to turn it around so it wouldn't mark the walls as I walked upstairs. I dragged this carrycot across the floor by the handles, my legs dragging along with it, as it was almost as tall as me. When I finally got there, I went to place the cot down beside Greg, but he told me no.

I quickly jumped back up, not knowing what he wanted me to do and worrying about what he might do to me if he thought I'd done it wrong.

He took the carrycot from me and went on to explain that because I was unable to settle George, he wanted me to hold my hands out in front of me. He was glaring down at me, making me feel incredibly overwhelmed and completely insignificant. I was confused about what was going to happen, but I also knew it wasn't going to be good. He then placed the carrycot in my hands and told me to hold it there, until he told me to stop. The carrycot was so heavy – how did he expect me to hold it?

With all my might I tried to hold the cot directly in front of me, but the sheer heaviness soon started to defeat me, my arms beginning to cave.

"Keep your arms straight," he scorned, "if you don't then you'll earn yourself a strike."

My arms felt like lead as they got heavier and heavier, and my upper arm muscles felt like they were ready to pop.

He always took pleasure in pronouncing the 'three strikes.' We had to live by this rule of three strikes, and when we reached our third, we would be 'punished'. Punished? Was I not already being punished?

I eventually caved – it just seemed impossible to hold this carrycot for any longer than a couple of minutes – and as tears streamed down my face the panic set in. I simply didn't know what to expect.

"I'm sorry, Greg," I timidly said in the hope that he would forgive me.

His face never changed; he appeared to always have the same eerie expression – a blank stare – every time he looked or talked to Sarah and me. Even if he was angry, I couldn't tell. He seemed to like watching us in pain and expected us to fail our tasks.

He spoke and I jolted. "From now on you both call me 'sir'. If I hear you call me Greg again then you will receive your strikes. Is that clear?"

"Yes sir," I cried.

He would explain that he was trying to toughen us up – that was his justification for the strikes. His justification for everything.

Holding the carrycot soon became a regular occurrence, and I always earned my strikes from dropping it. At this point he would shout for Sarah to come into the room, going on to give Sarah the same task whilst I stood there watching. Sarah was smaller than me, meaning that the cot was even larger for her to carry, but she did it; with all her might she attempted to lift this carrycot.

At times I wondered if she was stronger than me, which made it even harder for me to watch; I felt as though she would always have to pick up when I failed.

"Strike two!" he would say, like a drill sergeant. He always seemed to enjoy the authority he had over us and would wait in anticipation – like a child waiting for their sweets – for us to reach the third strike.

By this point we'd both be streaming in tears and all I wanted was my mummy. Where was Mummy? Why wasn't she here to save us from this monster?

When Mummy did return to the house, however,

we didn't dare tell her what had gone on. Surely, though, she knew what he was doing to us, would know something was wrong from our silence? We would both just sit together on the one single chair, our hands on our knees as commanded.

We became accustomed to composing ourselves this way at all times, our playful selves soon becoming a distant memory. We simply became too frightened to play, for fear of getting into trouble.

As the weekend neared, we'd be told to go and play outside. We were never given a time to be back in by, we were just told to knock and to wait for the door to be answered when we wanted to come back inside. We knew we weren't allowed to leave the square, but luckily for us there was a small park to the side of the second square, which Sarah and I would often play in.

I loved going to the park, and my favourite part was swinging on the swings. There were two, just enough for me and Sarah to have one swing each. They were old, with bright red seats and rusty old chains that intertwined perfectly as they wrapped around the rusty bar above. I would race Sarah to the swings to see who got there first, excited about being able to play.

Once seated, I would swing my legs up as far as I could, trying to reach the sky, but then I would stop and look upwards, often wondering whether the sky was descending down on me with solace, mercy or simply sadness, making me feel meaningless in this world. For a second all my problems would disappear as I concentrated on the cool wind blowing against my face, the sun beaming down whilst I squinted my eyes ever so harshly to look at the clouds and the sky above. It was too beautiful; the sky was like a royal-blue vessel wrapped in sparkles that flickered and dotted about like slush – or were these simply the drops of tears that would shower me for the foreseeable future? Then, as the swing came to a halt, all the fear and anxiety would hit back at me, landing on top of me like a ton of bricks.

Once Sarah and I became tiresome of the park, we would go and play games around the square, including the popular 'knock and run'. We would knock on random people's doors and then run as fast as we could. We had no idea who lived there – in fact, we didn't know any of our neighbours. This gave us our tiny bit of thrill, the only thrill that we ever got to experience, but not once did it occur to us that we might be caught.

This went on for months. Come rain or shine, we would randomly knock on doors and run as fast as we could, just to pass the time.

Spring days passed on towards the summer, and many times Sarah and I would sit on the doorstep of where we lived as it poured down with rain, having knocked to be let back in several times. This would go on for hours with no response, and we could only sit and wait. We were cold and wet, and nobody cared. We had run out of things to do and so we just sat there, two frail little girls waiting to be let in, out of the rain.

Then, one day as we returned home from playing our silly games, we only had to knock once, and he was there waiting for us. He'd heard what we'd been doing with the knock and run game and he ordered us back inside. As he calmly led us into the living room, he made us stand side by side and began to inform us of what he'd been told. He didn't look mad, there was just a slight crease around the corner of his mouth. He was pleased that we were about to be punished, and for something we'd actually done wrong.

We had disturbed him, I knew that much, as he'd never answered the door so promptly the whole time we'd lived there.

Approaching me and Sarah, he grabbed both of our shoulders and directed us to the living room wall. "Stand there on your tiptoes, noses touching the wall, until I say you can move," he ordered.

I faced the wall, standing side by side with Sarah, and began to think this wasn't so harsh. Were we being let off easily?

All I could hear in the background was the television, and so – just to pass the time – I would imagine myself sitting there watching it, as well as imagining how the characters might look. I could also hear Greg talking about the army and how he missed Mendez, as if the life he had now was tedious and without purpose.

His musings would remind me of Daddy, and so I would dream of my daddy coming in – dressed in his white shining armour – to rescue me and Sarah, to tell us he was taking us home. I would daydream about anything just to take my mind off the heavy feeling in my legs, my thighs, my calves. My toes had also started to cramp; I was sure I wouldn't be able to move them once I came away from the wall. We'd been standing there for what seemed like hours.

With each second that passed my feet began to crumble a little more, and I would try to rest them on the floor. He knew every time Sarah and I did this, however, as he would yell, "Feet up!" Was he watching us? Had he been watching us this whole time? How did he know?

Eventually he would let us go, though the time for dinner had come and gone and he would order us to bed with no tea. We were afraid that our mealtimes might be cancelled from now on.

In that moment, I didn't care much for eating, as

the pain in my legs was taking up all my thoughts – there was a burning sensation running up and down my calves, and they were incredibly stiff. Walking to the bedroom, I tried not to show that I was in pain; all I could think of was curling up in bed and resting my legs.

The following morning I awoke with anticipation, then slowly crawled out of bed and wandered to the living room. He was there again, sitting on the couch in his pale brown shorts, spread out on the sofa. I was hungry and could hear my stomach rumbling as I walked towards the single chair that Sarah and I had grown to loath.

"Go get your sister!" he barked.

"Yes sir," I replied. I hastily jumped from the sofa and ran to the bedroom to tell Sarah that he wanted her. Coming back, as I approached the couch I looked around, then closed my eyes and prayed that Mummy would walk in. Again, I didn't know where Mummy was, or why was she never here. All I knew was that I could sense something terrible was about to happen. We were all alone with Greg and George was in his carrycot, fast asleep. I could feel myself shaking with anticipation, worried about what he was going to say.

Then, without hesitation, he went on to explain that we needed to tidy up before Mummy got home. He explained that he wanted us to start at one end of the living room, picking up all the bits that were on the carpet.

This was new. Was the hoover broken? I asked myself as I bent down on all fours to start picking up the bits.

Greg stood up and checked his watch, then told us we had fifteen minutes to pick up all the bits from this dark brown carpet –and that he was going to time us.

Once again panic set in. I already knew it was an impossible task – Sarah and I were bound to miss something, especially with the timescale he'd given us – but what else could we do?

With Sarah and me at each end of the room, we hurriedly started to pick up what bits we could find. I didn't bother to look up to see how far Sarah had gotten, as I knew I wouldn't have time to waste.

"Time's up," he said, far sooner than I expected.

I paused what I was doing and began to stand up ever so slowly, knowing full well that I hadn't reached the other end of the room. I watched him walk slowly up and down the room, dragging his bare feet across the carpet and looking for any bits we'd missed.

Soon enough, he came across what he called 'dirt' and said those dreaded words: "Strike one."

I could hear Sarah starting to sniffle, as one by one the tears began to roll down her face. I wanted to tell her to stop as he hated it when we cried and it only seemed to increase his hatred of us, but I couldn't – I was too scared to even look properly at Sarah, let alone ask her to stop.

He wasn't finished, and I knew he was going to tell us to continue cleaning this huge carpet with our bare hands. And that he did, timing us again and watching over us as we struggled.

By now my eyes had started to fill up with tears, and with every breath I tried to hold them back, but all I could think of was where was Mummy. Inside my head, I begged and prayed for her to come home.

By this point I couldn't see any dirt on the carpet; I could barely even see the carpet through my tears, which had now started to stream down my face. I didn't dare wipe these away either, otherwise I'd lose any bits I'd already gathered in my hands.

"Strike two!" he yelped, his mean eyes raking over us scornfully. Clearly, he hadn't finished with us.

This time he didn't even bother to look for any unmissed bits on the carpet, but I could see that he was starting to get agitated, as he turned to Sarah and barked at her to stop crying. This only made her worse, jolting her where she stood. He began to walk towards her.

Grabbing her by the shoulder, he stormed her into the kitchen, and I followed – I knew by now that where Sarah stood, he also liked me to stand. As I followed, I thought of how I desperately wanted to get out of this place and go back to Nanny and Grandad's, or back to Germany – anywhere other than here.

Greg's face had now become even meaner than before, his hard gaze aimed at Sarah, his face becoming swollen whilst every inch of his body stiffened. I wasn't sure what he was going to do, or why he had marched Sarah into the kitchen. Was she at strike three already? He'd never said she was, so why was he so angry?

He reached over and turned on the cooker. I found myself mesmerised by the flames, still having no comprehension of what was about to happen.

He then grabbed Sarah's tiny wrist in the palm of his massive hand and shouted at Sarah to stop crying, giving her one final chance to stop.

Panic filled me as I prayed that she'd stop crying. I wanted to tell her – as her older sister – that it would be OK, but I could not. Was this because I was scared? Or because deep down, I knew it wasn't going to be OK? It wasn't going to be OK at all.

Before I could even finish my thoughts, her hand was over the fire.

I watched helplessly while she screamed, trying to pull her whole body away from him. She used all her might, kicking her little legs against the cooker to try and pull her hand away. His grip, however, was firm, and he kept her hand over the scorching flames as they touched the tips of her fingers.

I froze, crying, my whole body stiff, unable to move from where I stood, though my hands reached out to her from a distance, like I was trying to get her to come to me. I watched in horror, utterly helpless, as I knew I would get the same treatment if I attempted to prize this bully off my sister. I began to feel the anger raging inside me and I wanted to run over to Greg, punching him and screaming at him to get off her. But I could not; my body was firmly glued to the ground as my heart pounded through my chest. My mind was telling me to do one thing while my body was stopping me, full of fear.

I cried and I watched, but there was nothing more I could do. "I'm sorry," I whispered quietly, as Greg eventually let Sarah go.

He then stormed back into the living room, snorting while shaking his head, allowing Sarah to drop to the floor as she clenched her burnt hand with the other. By now she was both screaming and blowing quickly and repeatedly on her hand, in an attempt to cool it down. Her little hands clenched, broken like crumpled flowers that once flourished. To my shock, her hand was red raw, and as I watched, her thumb and the tips of her fingers began to blister.

Greg approached, picked Sarah up, and began to panic. Had he finally realised what he'd done?

Without hesitation, he phoned Mummy. I wasn't sure where she was, but within no time at all she was home and Sarah was rushed to the hospital.

I sat in the house, thinking of how Mummy would now know what he'd been doing, and how he was going to get into trouble. I wasn't sure how much trouble it would be, but being seven years old, I knew right from wrong.

Filled with reluctance and fear, I quietly waited for Mummy to return as I ran the story through my mind. I was going to tell her what that monster had done to us, and all the other things he did to us when she wasn't around, of how he was always mean to us. I imagined Mummy saying how sorry she was for leaving us with him, and opening her arms out to me, telling me that everything was going to be OK.

I don't remember anyone being in the flat with me that afternoon, whilst Mummy and he were at the hospital with Sarah – I couldn't say whether someone was there, or if I was alone – but I can tell you that I was trembling with shock when they both returned.

I watched as Greg reluctantly walked back into the living room, my body slowly shrivelling in his presence. Sharply, I lifted my eyes bravely to look at Mummy and saw her face screwed up from worry, her eyes saddened.

She didn't look back at me; her head was down as she focused on the floor. I could see her sheer concentration with every step she needed to take to get to the couch. She looked sad with despair.

I waited patiently for her to ask me my side of the story, but that never came. I was a fool for thinking she would – a big fool! I didn't know why Greg was still there, and I didn't ask, but soon enough the day came when I was finally allowed to visit Sarah in the hospital.

Before I could go, though, Greg grabbed my shoulder and led me to the small, dark bathroom. Then, not allowing me even one second to pause, he pulled down the toilet lid to sit on and turned me around, so I was facing him. I'd never been this close to his face before, and behind his glasses I could see his dark, lifeless eyes, cruel as death.

The more I investigated them the more hatred escaped from them, allowing me to truly see what kind of man he was.

His tone was quiet and placid as he began to dictate to me what I had to say about that dreaded day he'd burnt Sarah's hand. I was not under any circumstances allowed to express what I'd witnessed, otherwise he would kill the both of us.

I quickly nodded, moving my head vigorously up and down several times to emphasise my understanding of what he was saying. I wasn't going to say anything – how could I when he was there, watching my every move?

The hospital wasn't far from where we lived, and as I walked down the corridors I couldn't believe how magical the inside of the hospital looked – animal prints covered the walls and there were toys everywhere. Each hospital bed was lined up in a row, with a child either sitting on or lying down in their very own bed.

As we walked past the metal beds, I observed each one in the hope that I would spot Sarah. And then there she was, sitting just as dainty as the flowers on the bed, playing with her Barbie dolls. Her long bushy curly hair was what stood out from the rest of the children, though my attention went straight to her hand, which was all bandaged up. I could see, however, that she was alright due to the smile she gave me – the biggest smile I'd seen on her face in a long time.

We didn't stay long, and I didn't say anything; even though I wanted so desperately to scream out what had happened I knew I could not, for fear of what was going to happen to me.

After two long weeks Sarah returned home with

a rather unpleasant large see-through glove on her hand. This was well attached to her wrist and was much bigger than her hand itself. I took a closer look, surprised to see what seemed to be small drops (that looked like milk) dripping from her fingers and thumb into the bottom of the glove. I wasn't sure what to think of this, but all I knew was that whilst Sarah was recovering it was up to me to take the punishment for the both of us.

As the months went by the glove was removed from Sarah's hand and she was left with a scarred, deformed thumb, where her nail grew at an angle rather than perfectly straight. When Sarah turned her hand over to the palm side, you could see the burn marks that ran from the tip of her thumb right down to her wrist. It looked as though she had half a thumb. Sarah had to visit the hospital regularly to get skin grafts put onto her thumb, taken from her bottom, but this never seemed to faze Sarah. She was brave – probably the bravest of us all.

Me and Sarah were kept inside over these months, spending weeks and weeks cooped up in our bedroom. I would often sit by the window that looked directly onto our square and watch the people go about their daily lives. If I wasn't in my bedroom, I would be helping out at the off-licence Greg had started managing; I would help him fill the shelves and rip up the boxes, ready for disposal. This felt good because I was trying to show him that I could be useful – that I could help – and I also knew that whilst I was helping, he would leave me and Sarah alone. I wanted him to digest all the work I'd done and all the effort I'd put into helping him, hoping that he'd question the right and wrong of how he was treating us.

One evening, when Mummy had shouted for Sarah and me to have a bath, Greg appeared as we were getting ready to get unchanged, turning off the light to make the bathroom grim and dim. He stared at us while we stood to attention, putting the toilet seat down and bending down to sit on it.

"Now, your father is coming tomorrow to take you two for tea," he told us. "You are not to tell him anything that's going on here, otherwise you'll be in big trouble when you get back. Have I made myself clear?"

We both nodded fiercely and dramatically.

"What do you say?"

"Yes, sir," we both replied.

Despite Greg's warning, I could hardly contain my excitement that we were finally going to see Daddy. It had been so long since we'd seen our daddy that the only image I had of him was in his uniform, all in white, and I could not imagine him any other way.

CHAPTER THREE

THE TRUTH

SURE ENOUGH, WHEN he arrived to collect me and Sarah, he looked different. He seemed older and was no longer dressed in white. His hair no longer had curls either – it seemed to have thinned out – and he looked slightly chunkier around the waist compared to how I remembered him. I didn't mind, though; Sarah and I were spending the day with Daddy and that was all that mattered.

The journey in Daddy's car took about an hour, and when we arrived at his house, he introduced us to a blonde woman called Angela. With her was a small boy called Matthew. Daddy did not explain who they were, other than that he was living with them.

During that day we stayed in and talked to catch up, though it was mainly Daddy talking about how he'd come out of the army and was now working for himself as a gas man. Sarah and I couldn't really talk about much and so I found myself sitting in silence for most of the time we were at Daddy's.

I wanted to tell Daddy so much about what was going on, but fear struck me every time I went to open my mouth. I was constantly wrestling with both sides of my head – one side begging me to tell Daddy and the other screaming at me, 'No'! At the end of the day, I knew that Sarah and I would be returning home that very night and that we'd have to face Greg.

Before it was time to return home, Daddy told us that we could call him anytime and that all we needed to do was reverse the charges on the telephone and he would pay for the call. Daddy carefully wrote down his number on a piece of paper and explained to me in detail how to reverse the charges.

Did Daddy know that Greg was horrible to us? Was that why he was giving me his telephone number?

I knew I couldn't keep this piece of paper – what if Greg found it? – so now I had the challenge of memorising the number as quickly as I could on the journey home.

As we walked back through the square, I began to feel my legs twitching with nervousness. I just didn't want to go home. My inner self was screaming, 'Please Daddy, don't let us go back! Can you not see what has been happening to Sarah and me? Does no one know what that monster did to Sarah's hand?!'

As we walked, I carefully disposed of the piece of paper, hoping that Daddy wouldn't see me drop it. I had managed to memorise his number, and as soon as I got in, I would write it down somewhere using my felt tip pens, then hide it so no one knew I had it.

At this point we'd been living in that flat for a couple of years, and the blue front door was now chipped. I realised, as we got back from spending the day with Daddy, how much I hated that door. I had never really taken much notice of it before, but for some reason I now became mesmerised, staring at it deeply. My feet seemed nailed to the floor, and as I knocked on the door my knees started shaking nervously. I hoped no one was going to answer.

By now I was used to the door never being answered, as Sarah and I often sat at the door waiting to be let in (especially on the cold, dark days), but for some reason knocking on the door felt different this time. Standing in position, it seemed like a sacrificial offering. I prayed for it not to be answered – as then Daddy would have to take me and Sarah back home to his house – but, sure enough, Mummy answered the door and invited both me and Sarah in, insisting that we immediately make our way up to the living room. Sadly, we said our goodbyes to Daddy, relentlessly pondering how long it would be before we got to see him again.

I ran up to my bedroom as fast as I could (before Greg had time to notice I was back) so I could find a felt tip, a crayon, anything to write Daddy's number down. "Where is it?" I murmured to myself, trying to be as quiet and as quick as I could.

Rummaging through my toys, I eventually found a red felt tip pen, but then hesitation hit me as I found a crayon book. I slumped to the floor and tried to write down the first few numbers Daddy had given me. Was this right? In all the panic I was feeling, I wrote a number down, but was it Daddy's number? I couldn't remember.

With that thought, I heard Greg shouting for me to come into the living room. I nervously got up, asking myself whether he knew what I had done, and when I walked into the living room, I saw that Sarah was already there, standing by the couch. I placed myself next to her and then stared down at Greg, who looked so comfortable spread out on the couch, lying down with one leg hung over the edge. He had on those dreaded light brown shorts that he'd become accustomed to wearing, which I hated.

"What did you talk about whilst you were with your dad?" he scorned.

Sarah and I responded back with, "Nothing, sir," which was, in fact, the truth. I had wanted to tell Daddy everything, but I couldn't bring myself to do so. Did this make me a coward? Should I have been stronger for Sarah? After all, she was the one who bore the scars from him, she was the one who would have to look at her thumb for the rest of her life, being reminded of that terrible day.

For some reason, Greg didn't believe us. "That's strike one," he said. "Now, I'm going to ask you one more time: what did you tell your dad?"

Again, we repeated in harmony, "Nothing, sir."

By now I was both confused and upset, the tears beginning to swell my eyes. He'd told us not to say anything before we left, and now – even though we hadn't actually said anything – he didn't believe us. Were we in trouble? If that was the case, maybe I should have said something to Daddy after all. What was the point of staying silent if we were just going to be in trouble anyway?

Slowly, Greg sat up from the couch, clasping his hands together.

This was it, I thought to myself. We were in trouble anyway – for doing nothing.

Once up, he grabbed both of us by our shoulders and by our scruffs, holding us at arm's length like two diseased children he didn't want to touch. He then directed us to this small room between the bathroom and the living room. I never really gave this room much thought, as Mummy never felt it important to show us, but as he began to open the door, a slightly warm and moist breeze escaped from the room.

Inside there stood a big round cylinder covered in material with pipe work that poked out from either end, disappearing beneath the floor. "Strike two for the both of you, now you sit there," he scorned as he turned to Sarah and pointed to the ground where she was to sit. "And you there," he said to me as he forcefully pushed against my shoulder, directing me to sit opposite Sarah. He then ordered us both to stay there until we decided to tell the truth.

As he started to close the door behind him, the light from the hallway slowly began to diminish, until we were eventually both sitting in the dark.

"What's that?" Sarah screeched a moment later.

The cylinder was making rumbling sounds, like the belly of a pig as it announced its hunger. "It's OK, Sarah," I said, "it's just the boiler. It makes a funny sound, I think." I didn't really know, of course – how could I? – but I knew that, as the older sister, I needed to calm Sarah down to prevent us from getting into any more trouble. I, on the other hand, was not so scared, though I tried not to think about what stood between Sarah and me.

This overbearing boiler looked down on us as we curled up beside it at either end, our legs drawn up against our chests, clasping them tightly as so not to kick each other if we were to let go. You could almost hear a pin drop in there – that was, if it wasn't for the trickling sounds of water you could hear within the boiler. Its every sound was magnified, intensifying Sarah's whimper.

I tried to concentrate on the positive facts within that small, dingy room. At least, for instance, we weren't being watched. At least we were able to sit down and fall asleep if we wanted to, unlike when he made us stand on our tiptoes, facing the wall. It could definitely be worse.

"What are we going to do?" Sarah asked sheepishly and quietly, in the hope that she wouldn't be heard.

She was looking to me – her big sister – for answers, but the truth was, I had no idea. As the older one, I was supposed to come up with a solution, but I just had no clue what we were supposed to do.

We both threw some ideas back and forth, and we even considered lying to Greg, but that meant one of us would have to take on his wrath. Neither one of us wanted to take the punishment, and why should we? We hadn't done anything wrong.

We both sat there as quiet as mice, whispering to each other about how much we despised Greg until we had used every word imaginable (at least to two little girls) to describe him – words like horrible, monster, disgusting. None of them seemed strong enough.

After what felt like forever the door flung open and we were ordered out of the cupboard. To my amazement it was still light outside; I thought I'd been in that dingy room for hours and had been certain it would soon be bedtime.

As I began to unravel my stiff body from the cupboard to stand up, the realisation of it not being bedtime hit me right in the chest. My heart started to pound, as I fought so hard to contain the tears that were yet to fall.

Greg gnashed his teeth, as once again he began to ask whether we wanted to tell the truth. It was then that I felt a surge of uncertainty explode from within.

"Nothing!" I fired back. I glanced quickly at my sister who looked even frailer than I felt, shivering in his presence, standing frozen and staring at me wide-eyed. At that moment it struck me – both the words that had leapt from my mouth and the roaring hatred that was so clear in my voice. What had I done? I was sure I was going to be punished now.

I gulped at the sound of, "Strike three, come with me."

Greg walked very calmly back into the living

room, and as I followed I saw disaster looming in my future, like a ghostly figure hovering around us.

"We are going to have a fight," he told me.

A fight? What did he mean?

He began to move the couch back towards the end of the living room, whilst carefully placing the coffee table next to it, leaving a large, clear floor area. He then slumped to his knees, as cold and as solid as a lump of clay.

Sarah and I, who were once again standing side by side, were very confused. I could almost taste the fear and confusion in my mouth as my heart was pounding away, trying to escape.

Then I heard Mummy's quiet voice, a thin shrill voice, like the cry of an expiring mouse, ask, "What are you doing?"

Finally, Mummy was going to allow us to go to bed! After all, if Mummy didn't know what he was doing, then how were we supposed to know?

"I am going to teach the girls how to fight," he replied. "When they turn sixteen, they will have to move out and fend for themselves." He then removed his glasses, stretched his arm out in the direction of Mummy – silently expressing that she was to take these from him – and said, "Who's first?"

Even as anguish took hold of me, I knew it was

only fair that I stood forward in acknowledgment that I would go first.

"Well, come on then," spat Greg, "you have all that bravery to shout at me, so let's see how hard you can punch!"

With every inch of my body feeling like lead, I slowly walked towards him. I didn't know what I was going to do. I didn't know how we'd got to this stage.

I didn't like looking at this man, let alone touching him, and as I approached, I became face-to-face with this… monster.

Without hesitation, he grabbed my hair and began to pull on it, so that my head was forced to turn, facing away from him. With all the might I had, I began to punch in and around his arms – though they felt like hard rock – just to get him off my hair. My eyes began to stream with pitiful tears; I knew this was a losing battle before it had even begun.

He laughed continuously, enjoying my torment and my pathetic attempt to even get his hands off from around my hair. I was shaking and trembling with fear as I watched his small grin transformed into a wide, brutal smirk of destruction. I knew he hated the crying, but I just couldn't stop myself.

Then, suddenly, I was dropped down on the floor, like unwanted trash. I had gone from standing face-to-face with him, to lying on the floor, staring up at him.

With one hand still in the midst of my matted hair, he placed the other over my mouth and nose. I couldn't breathe. I tried to free myself by kicking my tiny legs up towards his overbearing body, but it was no good.

This feeling of not being able to breathe soared through my body as I tried to scream, "Mummy, Mummy, please!" I tried with all my might to free his hand – but it was just covered so firmly over my mouth and nose. I was panicking now, not knowing when I'd be able to breathe again.

Then, much to my surprise, he freed me.

I gasped for air, feeling my hot sweaty cheeks as I removed my sweat-soaked hair from around my eyes and face. I didn't dare move from my position.

"Are you just going to stand there or are you going to help your sister?" he snapped. I knew he was talking to Sarah, but I wasn't sure if I should be happy or sad about that, as all I could think about was what had just happened. I simply could not endure another episode of not being able to breathe.

Sarah didn't cry as she walked over to Greg, and then – much to my surprise – she proceeded to punch Greg around his arms and shoulders. I was also surprised at the sheer anger that Sarah portrayed in each punch. He continued to laugh, but this laugh was different from the laugh he gave me.

It was like Sarah had been waiting for permission to hit him, slamming all the years of torment he had given us into every punch. I continued to watch, hoping that she had diverted enough of his attention away from me, that he would forget I was lying there on the floor, feeling hopeless and defeated.

"Enough!" he laughed, and Sarah came to a sudden halt. She stared hard into his eyes, the expression on her face telling him that she didn't want to, as if she was sorry she had to stop.

As he ordered me onto my feet I wondered where all her strength had come from. She hadn't whimpered once compared to me, and I just wanted to tuck myself away tightly in the hope that I would just disappear.

"You can thank your sister for saving you this time," he said, before adding, "now you can both go to bed."

"Thank you," I quietly whispered to Sarah, walking as quickly as we could to our room before he changed his mind.

I was glad to be in there, though we never felt safe even when we were in our own bedroom. I dried my tears from my sweaty face and climbed into bed.

I would often get into bed and try to get to sleep as quickly as I could, but that night we both giggled at how Sarah had looked so mean, throwing her punches at him with the rage of a roaring tiger.

CHAPTER FOUR

HUNGER

WE DREAMED THAT, one day, we would both be able to beat him to the ground and show him how it felt to be bullied and to live in fear.

I lay my head on the pillow next to Sarah's, and I must have drifted off to sleep, as I suddenly awoke to a very slight shuffling sound, as though someone was walking across our bedroom floor.

I lay frozen, not daring to look; I knew it was him.

Whenever I heard him come into our room, I would stay beneath the covers as quietly as I could, trying not to draw any attention to myself.

It was dark outside. What could he possibly be doing?

Every breath I took became shallower and shallower, as I knew that even the slightest sound would remind him we were there. It was harder than I thought to try and keep every inch of my body still (so as not to be noticed), but I tried anyway.

He would come into our room many nights – when Sarah and I were in bed – and stare out of our window, using a pair of binoculars to peer into the flats and shops opposite. I never cared to question or think about what he was doing. As long as he left soon – that was all I ever cared about.

With my breath held, my eyes shut tight, and my body stiff, I would lay like a corpse, invisible, so as not to be noticed.

I must have fallen asleep again, because the next thing I knew was Mummy waking me up, telling me to get up and get dressed, and to go and get some milk before school. It was still dark, and the frigid air had a cold snap that lingered like a corpse, encouraging me to want to stay under the duvet. But I got out of bed, hurriedly getting dressed as quick as I could to stay warm.

The butchers weren't far from the house – just a short distance across the square – and this was my regular place for getting milk. I never knew the man's name that served me each morning, but he seemed to know me, as he always greeted me with a smile and a, 'Morning, Kelly!' I went there as it was the only place open so early in the morning. Every time I went, I would do so quickly; my lingering conscious would be screaming at me to be as fast as possible, to avoid any trouble from the monster that awaited me back home.

On our way to school, Sarah and I discussed him. As it turned out, I'd been concentrating so hard on keeping myself quiet the night before, that I'd had no idea that Sarah had been awake the whole time and had also witnessed him entering our room. She was good, I thought to myself. Even after he'd left our room, neither one of us dared to look to check he wasn't there, instead staying as still and quiet as possible until we drifted back to sleep.

The days at school seemed bleak. I don't recall learning anything or remember any details of the subjects I took. I simply lived in fear – that's what I had become accustomed to. No matter how hard I tried, I could not shut out this darkness. This unknown world was as wild as primeval chaos, my fear and anxiety hanging around me like a dark, impenetrable cloud.

Was every home like this? Did all children have to endure the torture that me and my sister suffered? Eventually this was my way of thinking. As no one came to help us or take us out of this situation – not even Mummy – it pealed through my brain that this must be normal.

Returning home after school, Sarah and I often found ourselves alone for the first couple of hours, looking after our brother George. As much as I loved George, I loathed him as well. He was Greg's child, always managing to escape any punishment given to me and Sarah. With anything George did wrong, it was me and my sister who suffered the consequences. So, when we were alone with George, we would do all we could to keep our eye on him – and to keep him quiet.

One of the things we would do was play with his cars up and down the coffee table, with George sitting at one end and either me or Sarah sitting at the other. We would push the cars along, making all sorts of crazy car sounds, just to keep him occupied. Nothing held his interest for long.

He was a restless soul, detached, an unceasing shadow searching for anything better to do, as he never liked to sit still. "I don't like this game anymore," he wailed once as he ran at the big brown cabinet and began to climb.

"Get down from there!" I scolded, conscious that – as the cabinet began to lean forward like the tower of Pisa – it could fall and tumble on top of him.

The unwanted anticipation grimly crept in, as we waited for either Mummy or 'him' to return home. I prayed that Mummy would be first home and would relieve me from the pressures of George. When Mummy finally returned, however, she proceeded to the kitchen to commence dinner.

I never spoke to Mummy anymore; I didn't really even notice her. She had become this dark figure that lingered in the background, providing us with just the bare necessities for survival.

Then, in the midst of Mummy cooking, he returned.

He must have been home a while, as when he approached the coffee table he already had on the brown shorts he so loved to wear. He turned on me like a thunder cloud. "Who's moved my bottle on the shelf?" he scorned, pointing at and then repositioning the bottle on the big brown wooden case that stood aimlessly in the living room.

"George was climbing the shelf, sir," I sheepishly replied, with a shallow, broken voice.

"What have I told you about keeping him away from this shelf? Are we not at strike three by now?" he asked chillingly, smiling as if saying those words was the highlight of his day.

The tears were once again falling down my face; he could summon my tears as if he were summoning servants.

"Get up!" he yelled, and with that I followed him straight into the kitchen.

Reaching into the cupboard, he pulled out the chilli powder, and I stood there like a little lost child, not wanting to place my eyes upon him. Instead I dropped my gaze towards the floor, too scared to look up.

Then, intently listening to him pulling cutlery from the drawer, I raised my head to see him pointing a spoon at me.

"Open," he said, compounding his mean words with hard eyes. I knew he was telling me to open my mouth.

He placed the chilli powder onto the spoon carefully, so as to not spill any, and then rammed it into my mouth, telling me to swallow. It was fiery and spicy, and it burned my mouth and throat as I swallowed, the sharp and unpleasant taste bringing me instantly to tears. My nose streamed and panic set in; I felt as though his fingers were curling around my neck, pressing tight as I began to choke on my own saliva – which wouldn't wash the taste away from my mouth. Then, before I knew what was happening, another spoonful approached and was forced into my mouth. Desperation to breathe overtook me.

My face and throat both felt like they were under immense pressure, and unable to bear even thinking about swallowing the chilli powder, I held it in my mouth, where it burnt my tongue.

"Get it swallowed, four eyes, and don't be sick or

you'll earn yourself another strike!" he howled, clasping my cheeks with his fingers and squeezing my face to ensure that every bit of residue was swallowed.

Then, like hunted prey that couldn't flee, I began to swallow it. My throat muscles tightened, rejecting this ghastly taste as I tried to force it down. It was no good – I couldn't bear another spoonful. I was already standing there like a beaten rock, defeated. And why was he calling me four eyes anyway?

I continued to wail as my cheeks cooled from the tears now rolling down my face. I thought I might die from the hotness that surrounded my mouth – but then, again, what if I *did* die? Would Mummy feel sorry? Would she be full of regret? Would she even cry?

After all, Mummy was there in the room with us – had been this entire time – and she'd done absolutely nothing to stop Greg, to stop this madness. She simply continued to peel potatoes as though nothing was happening.

My watery eyes laid upon her for solidarity. Please Mummy, I thought, look at me! Can you not see what this monster of a man is doing to me? But there was nothing; she just continued to go about her daily business, like I was nothing more than a shadow of her past. Perhaps she would only be too happy to get rid of me. Perhaps that's what she actually wanted.

As I was staring at my mother, the tears still rolling down my face, Greg ordered me to go to bed.

On the way I walked past an incredibly pale-looking Sarah; she'd been watching, had seen the whole thing. In that moment I hated him so much, not only because of what he was doing to Sarah and me, but for the mean ugly words that constantly gushed from that mouth of his.

My distraught thoughts suddenly took to being wild. I wanted to escape from this place and seek out happiness, somewhere I wouldn't cry for at least one day. Was there such a place for me? I wondered.

I placed myself in bed, aware of the fact that I had the aftertaste of chilli powder in my mouth, along with a feeling of pure emptiness deep down in my belly. This hunger had recently appeared, and it had become my constant fellow traveller, causing me to have sharp stabs of pain. Was I not to have dinner again?

Closing my eyes, I placed my thumb in my mouth, trying to shut out his hateful face – a face that so coldly screamed at me as I lay there, helpless.

I awoke in the middle of the night to silence, Sarah lying beside me. It must have been the middle of the night, though I wasn't aware of the time – I never was, I only knew daylight and night-time. I didn't own a clock or a watch; I only had the silence to go on. My life screamed with silence, like a forgotten melody that only spoke or moved when told to do so.

Slowly, I arose from bed to look outside my big bay window, seeing if the shops were open – this would give me at least some indication as to whether it was close to morning.

As I peered out of the window my belly began to rumble, like the sound of faraway thunder or an old-fashioned train approaching from the distance.

"Kelly, what are you doing?" Sarah whispered suddenly.

"I don't know what time it is and I'm hungry," I replied, just as quietly.

"OK, let's go and get something to eat," she said softly as she crept out of bed.

Quietly opening our bedroom door so as not to make a sound, we slowly walked through to the kitchen, but after opening all the cupboards to look for something to eat, it soon became apparent that I couldn't take any food that would be missed. So, what seemed like a great idea at the time from my sister, soon turned into the realisation that I would just have to wait until breakfast.

But then I decided to look in the bin.

As gross as this may sound, I was *so* hungry, and after what felt like a lifetime of not eating, I would eat anything just to stop the pains that were roaring around in my belly.

After rummaging for a bit, I saw the potato peel that Mummy had thrown in earlier. I began to pick this up and as I did so, Sarah copied me. With a handful of potato peels in each of our hands we walked quietly back to our bedroom, hoping no one would notice the peels missing from the bin.

We sat on the bed for a moment, hungrily apprais-ing the raw unwashed potato peels, and then we both placed them into our mouths. They had a sweetish taste and didn't taste that bad. In fact, my mind and my belly very much appreciated this succulence in this time of hunger.

We giggled together that night as we realised that not only had we done something mischievous, but we'd got away with it too. We decided that night that when-ever Mummy cooked potatoes we would collect the potato peels from the bin and save them for when we were hungry. But where, we asked ourselves, were we going to stash this emergency food for when we needed it? I looked around the bedroom, soon finding an open-ing to the carpet right at the end of the room.

"Here, Sarah, let's put the leftovers under the carpet; he'll never find it here," I said. We were giggling away like the two little schoolgirls we were, as though we'd just stolen a load of candy from the shops.

The realisation of going hungry got me thinking. I despised the fact that we had to eat from the kitchen bin, and after a while I was tired of eating potato peels. I knew that this was going to become a regular occurrence, and I also knew something needed to be done about it.

So, one day on my way back from school, I told Sarah my idea of going into the shops below the flats to grab some food, which we could stash in our bedroom for whenever we were sent to bed with nothing to eat. She agreed.

Entering the shop that I was so familiar with; I began to scour the aisles. Nervous, I began to imagine that everyone knew why I had come into the shop. My fingers trembled as I picked up some bread and placed it down again, like I was anticipating buying it. Realising that a loaf of bread would be too big to get out of the shop unseen, however, I headed to the chocolate aisle instead.

With Sarah by my side, I told her to keep a lookout; to watch what the shopkeeper was doing and to let me know if he looked our way. Then, like mice that stole in and out, I carefully picked up a bar of chocolate to place in the sleeve of my jumper.

"Let's go," I whispered to Sarah.

We ran out of the shop and around the corner, where I showed Sarah the prize I'd managed to get.

"You only got one chocolate?" she asked, sighing in disappointment.

"Yes, sorry," I replied, "it's my first time doing this; I'll do better next time."

I opened the bar of chocolate and gave half to Sarah. It felt so good to eat, the texture, the chocolate melting in your mouth... it had been so long since we'd had anything so nice and sweet. We knew we had to be quick, though, and once we'd eaten it, we checked each other's mouths for any leftover evidence of chocolate around our faces, to make sure we wouldn't get caught.

That evening when we returned home, he was waiting for us, the blood from his face drained. "Where have you been?" he asked.

I heard Sarah whimper – clearly, she was worried that we'd been caught – but before I could say anything, he dragged me by my hair, pulling me into the kitchen.

I leaned to one side, crouching further to the floor and clutching my head with one hand to try and relieve the pain he was inflicting.

Releasing my hair, he opened the kitchen cupboard above his head, demanding to know who took the chocolate bar from the cupboard.

I looked to Sarah, assuming it must have been her. After all, I knew I hadn't taken it. There was a frightened look in her eyes, and she looked to me to be her saviour.

"I don't know, sir," I responded frantically.

He looked at Sarah, walking towards her as he screamed, "Well?"

By now she was crying, trying desperately to wipe the tears away with her hand and flinching with every move he made in her direction. I watched him place his hands on her hair to drag her in my direction, and without a second thought I screamed out, "It was me!"

I had never seen him this angry before; whenever we usually received our punishment, he seemed cool, calm, and collected, like his every move was carefully planned and calculated. But he didn't calculate this – he'd never anticipated that a chocolate bar would be stolen from the kitchen cupboards, especially as it was a cupboard that neither me nor Sarah could reach.

With one swing from his fist he punched me in the face. I didn't even have time to move out the way.

I fell to the floor clutching at my left eye, which felt as though it was ready to pop, and screamed out as I continued to cry in pain, certain that I would lose it.

As I wailed Greg walked to the freezer to grab a bag of peas, firmly handing it over to me and demanding I place it over my eye. Then, once I had managed to numb the pain from the throbbing, he made us stand by the living room window to wait for Mummy to return home, so that we could tell her what we did. I continued to hold the bag to my eye and prayed that Mummy would return soon. All I wanted to do was sleep – I was exhausted, and the constant standing to attention was making me weak.

Finally, Mummy returned home, a look of exhaustion and confusion riddling her face. She turned to Greg and asked what had gone on.

"Your girls have been stealing; there's a chocolate bar missing from the cupboard," he told her.

"A club?" Mummy asked, clearly knowing what chocolate he was talking about.

"Yes."

"No, Greg – I took one to work with me this morning," she explained.

As she spoke a surge of relief washed over me. I couldn't believe what I was hearing. Sarah hadn't taken it after all; it was Mummy, and he'd accused us!

He turned his head away from Mummy and rose to look over at us, an inhumane smirk on his face. "Looks like I owe you an apology," he said, not sounding sorry at all. "I suppose you want to go to bed now?"

I nodded slowly in response. By now my head was pounding and all I wanted to do was sleep it off. I didn't care that we'd go hungry again with no tea. I was no longer hungry anyway; it would be another night of potato peel for Sarah if she was.

The mornings became monotonous and repetitive, as each morning in the cold I would walk to get the milk before getting ready for school.

The man at the butchers where I got the milk from was the first to notice my black eye. “What’s happened to your eye, Kelly?” he asked, his own eyes bulging in a pitiful way.

“My brother hit me in the face with a chess piece and it caught my eye,” I told him. I had been trained to lie about anything that Greg was doing to us at home. This particular story he had drilled into me, again in the dull, dark bathroom, sitting upon the toilet seat where he loved to have his little talks with us. If I didn’t lie, the consequences would be far worse, he told me. I believed him.

By now George was getting older, and it was our job as his sisters to walk him to school.

By day I would dream. I didn’t care much for school, I didn’t care much for anyone, as no one cared much for me. I pondered the direction of my thinking, when my dreams were striking and attractive. Dreams that would simple lead me into so much trouble, but I didn’t care – the daydreams were mine and no one could take them away from me. I could imagine being rescued by my daddy and not living in fear every time I had to go home. I could imagine him taking me swimming and to the fairground, where I would go on all the rides. But daydreams were simply impotent, insignificant in my world, and I would quickly return back to truth, back into reality.

Would I ever be happy? Had God written this path for me – an eternal certainty to live in fear each day, each hour, minute, seconds? Was happiness a possibility or was this dreaded life going to be my fate? No. All we had was each other – Sarah and me – and hope. Hope that one day Daddy would come and take us away from that horrible man.

We continued like savages, having to scrounge for food out of the kitchen bin whenever Mummy cooked potatoes. I also continued to steal chocolate bars from the shop, to eat after school, on most days. I made sure to always eat everything in my packed lunch in case my evening meal was rationed to nothing, though our lunches were nothing to be ecstatic about. It would always be the same: a jam sandwich and a packet of crisps. No chocolate ever! I always craved something more, and whenever I saw my friends have a piece of cake or something else sweet added to their packed lunch, jealousy would overrule me. This pushed me further to continue stealing chocolate from the shop, even though I knew it was wrong. I was just so hungry most days, and if I thought I could have gotten away with stealing proper food, I would have done.

CHAPTER FIVE

A CRY FOR HELP

THEN, SUDDENLY, MY thoughts came yapping and growling, surrounding me like a pack of wolves. I knew what I had to do.

I was going to call my daddy and do what he told me: reverse the charges. I just had to go home, get the number, and then wait until I was ordered out of the house, when I could make the phone call. We had a telephone in our home, right above the round kitchen table, and although there were so many times I wanted to use this to call Daddy, fear stopped me in my tracks every time – fear of Greg, and what he'd do to me when he found out. Which he most definitely would.

So, when the opportunity arose – when he would inevitably kick us out to play – I planned to go to the telephone box at the end of the square.

I would tell Daddy everything that was going on, he would believe me, and he would come and rescue us from this wretched house straight away. I told Sarah about my cunning yet scary plan to call Daddy, and she agreed, excited.

"Out!" Greg ordered, and with that, Sarah and I quickly ran to our bedroom to put our shoes and coats on – and to grab Daddy's number that I had so carefully stored.

As we quietly walked down the stairs to the front door, I could feel the excitement running through me; it was like all my Christmases had come at once. I couldn't wait to get to the phone box, which was located at the end of the square just at the entrance to our block of flats. The first part of our mission was to go down the stairs and get to the phone box without being seen.

As we walked along the outskirts of the square, we didn't dare look back – we just kept going until we reached the red phone box, like a pair of bulls charging with fury to reach the red cape. Then, combining our strength, we opened the heavy glass door to the telephone box. We'd made it.

Squeezing inside together, I reached up to lift the phone off the hook, my thoughts turning to Daddy as all my hope bloomed inside me. As I dialled one hundred to reverse the charges, my every move was carefully thought out so as not to make a mistake.

It was important that I got through to Daddy; I thought that even if I did get found out, it would all be worth it once I'd spoken to him.

"Hello, how can I help you?" a woman's voice said softly on the other end, sounding nice and welcoming.

"Hello," I said, my voice stuttering and crackling due to the surprise of a woman answering. Daddy didn't tell me about this bit. After taking a deep breath I continued to say, "I want to call my daddy."

"OK," said the woman, "if you have your daddy's telephone number and your name, I will put you through."

"Yes, it's Kelly," I replied in an excited, screeching voice.

Within seconds of me reading the telephone number to her, the phone started to ring.

"Hello," said Daddy, and I quickly replied, "Daddy, it's me," but before I could finish the lady started speaking again.

"Do you except the reverse charges from Kelly?" she asked him.

"Yes, of course," he replied.

Relief ran through me. "Hello Daddy, it's Kelly," I said, very nervously.

"Hello Kelly, how are you?"

"I'm OK," I said slowly, before adding, "Sarah is here with me and we both want to speak to you."

"OK, fire away," he replied.

I began to gabble and splutter, all the while wondering if Daddy was making any sense of what I was saying. "Greg is mean to me and Sarah and we want to come and live with you," I finished.

As Daddy began to reply Sarah started tapping me on the shoulder as she jumped up and down, eager to hear and know what Daddy was saying.

"Stop it, Sarah, I'm trying to talk to Daddy," I told her.

There was a brief pause in conversation then, leading me to check whether Daddy was still there.

"Yes Kelly, I'm still here," he said slowly. "Look, I'm sure Greg doesn't mean to be mean, and I'm afraid – at the moment – that you can't come and live with me. I have no room, and besides, I would have to talk to Mummy first," he explained with his firm voice that seemed to puncture through the ceiling of the phone box.

Without hesitation I pounced back and said, "No, please don't tell Mummy we called you; I don't want to get into trouble."

In that instant, Sarah turned her back to me and started staring out of the glass box. I could tell she was disappointed as she started to blow her warm breath onto the glass, drawing a heart shape in the centre of the mist.

"Well," I said quietly, "when can we see you again?"

"Soon, I promise," he replied, pausing for a moment before saying, "I tell you what, how about I start writing to you? That way we can stay in touch all the time and I can talk to you about my days and what I'm doing. What do you think?"

Reluctantly, I agreed. "OK, Daddy," I said sadly. "Well, I have to go now. I'll speak to you soon." Now that I knew Daddy wasn't coming to get us, I didn't want to be seen huddled in this phone box and get into any more trouble. "Bye Daddy."

As I hung up, I just stared at the back of the phone box, numb.

I wasn't as eager to get back home as I'd been to get to the telephone box. The man I'd seen as my saviour was gone – now I saw him as my foe. If Daddy wasn't going to help us, then who would?

My life was flowing away like a river as I lost more and more of myself. After all, Greg kept reminding us both that once we turned sixteen, we were going to be kicked out of the house. Retiring from the phone box we did not say a word to each other. A deep twisted feeling in my gut became my constant reminder, that we were to accept our bleak future.

We continued to walk around aimlessly, like little lost puppies that had walked too far from home and had lost their bearings. Only we knew exactly where we lived, so we sheepishly started to walk home, ready to sit outside and wait to be let in.

The minutes turned into hours, with our bodies curled up against the dreaded blue door on the doorstep, our arms and legs drawn into our chests in an attempt to keep warm.

Eventually, the door opened. "Get in," he stated flatly.

We'd just started trampling our defeated hearts and bodies upstairs – with the sole intent to go to the one place where we had some solace, our bedroom – when he glared at us, telling us to go into the living room. He wanted to fight again. Only this time the duvet from our bed was there on the living room floor. He'd been preparing this very moment for us while we'd been freezing outside.

My heart was fluttering madly as I watched him kneel on my blanket, carefully removing his glasses so as not to break them.

"Well, come on then, four eyes!" he spat, placing his cold hollow eyes upon mine like an unwanted thundercloud.

Every inch of my body screamed at me to stay put, as the unwanted memories of my last fight crept in like a snail. This felt like punishment, but I hadn't earnt my three strikes, so why had I been summoned to such a task that made every inch of my body cry out?

As I neared him, my legs turned to jelly. Then, with my fist as tight as I could possibly make it, I swung that first feeble punch towards his shoulder as he sat there kneeling, looking as bald as a hawk. He returned the favour with a callous slap across my tiny face, which stung as though it were frozen. With the sheer shock and sting of that malicious slap, he once again summoned my tears like the drill sergeant he portrayed himself to be.

I caved in, dropping my hand to my side as he grabbed my throat with his right hand. "What's the matter, four eyes? Are you not even going to try and release my grip from your throat?" he taunted, coldly staring into my teary eyes. He was enjoying this, knowing full well that a girl of my size stood no chance of being able to defeat him.

He swayed in a sudden grip of anger as I continued to cry, allowing my beads of tears to fall down my face moment by moment, rolling down my chin and drenching his grip. I did not respond to his question. Every inch of my inner self was praying that he would summon Sarah to join in the fight and release me from his tormented grip. I could not withdraw my sobs, even though I knew he despised the crying.

His stare became even colder as he seethed through his teeth, and then he released his grip from my throat – but only to replace it on my hair.

Before I knew it I had been pulled to the ground, where I was once again facing this evil monster looming down at me from above. I didn't have time to comprehend what he was doing, but I could hear his knees cracking as he slowly stood up, whilst I began to wipe the wetness of the tears from my face. He grabbed my hair and ankles then, sliding me along the duvet to the edge, and my stiff body lay still as he began to roll me up inside the duvet, covering me from head to toe. I just lay there, my body broken.

He placed his heavyweight body upon mine and shouted, "Now, get out of this!"

My sobs began to punch through me again as I lay there, bound and helpless. All I could see was darkness, and I felt like I was drowning in my own feelings of suffocation.

Panic set in, and I tried to wiggle my body away from him and the duvet. I wanted to feel the air on my face. I wanted to be free.

I began to feel the overbearing warmth strike over my body as I attempted to move and get out of the duvet. I cried profusely whilst screaming his unworthy name for help.

I couldn't breathe.

This was it, I thought to myself.

Why was he doing this? Why did he seek out the constant 'pleasure' of tormenting me and Sarah? He didn't like the crying, yet he did everything in his power to ensure that crying became an everyday way of life for Sarah and me.

My breath – what little air I had left – became warm as it increased. Then, suddenly, after what felt like an eternity of being wrapped up in the duvet, he released me.

The cool air swarmed at me like a colony of bees as I swiftly removed myself from the duvet, so as not to encourage him to place me there again.

To my surprise, as I pulled my damp hair away from my flushed face, I saw Mummy standing there beside Sarah. Greg turned his hard flint eyes on Mummy and Sarah and smugly said, "Come on then, I'm waiting." He was talking to Mummy.

Standing like a carved figure so that I wouldn't draw attention to myself, I wondered what had been said whilst I'd been trying to fight my way out from his cruel little game.

His face grew very grim as Mummy seemed to shrink in his presence. She took off her shoes, her face turning waxen white with every slow step as she creeped towards him.

She was going to fight him instead.

Finally, she was going to release me and Sarah from his clutches and what seemed like our daily duty.

I stood and watched as Mummy put the full force of her body onto his, though as they wrestled, I was sure he was going easy on her. It hardly seemed fair. Why would he not show Mummy how ruthless he was with Sarah and me?

He laughed at Mummy's attempts to wrestle him to the ground. She was becoming flustered, her hair matted as she fought her way from the ground to get above him.

I didn't know how I felt watching Mummy and Greg fight. On the one hand, I was pleased that Mummy had rescued me from the panic-stricken feeling I'd been experiencing when wrapped up in the duvet. After all, now she would know how it felt to fear his actions and feel the force of his grip. But then I also felt sorry for her. Did she feel it was her duty to help us? Did she even want to fight him?

As time passed and the exhaustion overruled both Mummy and Greg, he ordered Sarah and me to the wall. By now he didn't need to explain what this involved, as we automatically stood on our tiptoes, our noses touching the wall. Oh, how I despised this wall.

When would we be allowed to go bed? I wondered. Bed became my only solace, the only place and the only thing I could depend on – and even that was debatable.

Normally I would find comfort with my duvet, wrapping it around me from head to toe. I would twizzle the corner of my pillow in between the fingers of one hand, placing my thumb from my other hand into my mouth to suckle while I rocked myself to sleep. I didn't care much for eating tea, not now I had my secret stash of potato peel that I would sneak from the bin every time Mummy cooked a meal involving potatoes. And I didn't care for watching television either, as I always felt like I was on tenterhooks whenever I was around him, in fear that I would earn a strike for just breathing.

I stood looking aimlessly at the wall, not knowing whether there was a point to all this. It was uncomfortable standing up against the wall, and it took a lot of concentration and willpower to ensure that I stayed on my tiptoes. How I yearned to be in the boiler cupboard right now!

I would often find myself cross-eyed, looking at the same spot of wallpaper for hours. If I didn't do this, then I would find myself drawn to the temptation of wanting to close my eyes, which would be bad for me. I would no longer dream of the days when Daddy would come for us, or for Mummy to save us. In fact, by now Mummy had almost become a distant memory, a dark shadow that remained in the background and only appeared to me unexpectantly, in certain times of need.

I rarely spoke to Mummy; she always seemed too busy to notice us. Sarah and I hardly spoke around the home at all, in fact, unless it was to each other, and as long as we could be sure we weren't within earshot of Greg.

I'd started to grow accustomed to this way of life; this was it for me and Sarah.

No one noticed anything wrong with us, which confirmed to me that the punishment we received must be normal in every household.

George, however, was treated differently. He could play in the living room, run around the living room, and even jump from couch to couch – all the things I wished I could do without feeling uneasy. George never had to do the chores that Sarah and I had to do, and he certainly wasn't given the three strikes rule to abide by. George was growing up to become quite handsome, with his striking blond hair that lay straight above his shiny blue eyes. Even though I loved George, however, I started to become envious of him, and wondered why he didn't have to stand against the wall or fight the evil like we did.

We were finally told it was time for bed, and relief rushed over me as I removed myself from the wall and walked swiftly to our bedroom. I proceeded to get undressed and into bed as Sarah asked, with pity, if I was hungry. I replied with a sharp, 'No'. I didn't care to eat any of the potato peel we had stashed; standing up against the wall after a drawn-out fight had tired me out, and all I wanted to do now was suck my thumb and go to sleep.

The next morning was like any other morning; I got up to go and get the milk and then headed to school. My school days were becoming nothing more than a haze. I spent most of my time looking for a clock, so that I would know how long I had left until home time. I began to teach myself the time, and I knew that when the clock struck three and the bell went, it was time to go.

I had a couple of friends at school, but I was never allowed to go to theirs for tea after school and they were certainly never allowed to come to mine. It never really entered my head to discuss my home life with any of my friends, simply because they never asked. I wouldn't dare tell them that Greg was mean anyway, as many people knew him, what with him working in the local off-licence.

"Right everyone, leave your homework on the table before you leave," my teacher said.

Homework! I couldn't do homework or find the time to do any homework, as Greg never took any interest in this. He was only interested in punishing us all the time.

Palpitations in my chest would start every time that school bell went, as I anticipated what was waiting for me at home. Opening the front door to let ourselves into the house, I would silently pray that he wouldn't be there. But most times he was, and once again it felt as though my prayers had gone unanswered. I was unsure who or what I was praying to, but I would always pray for no one to be home when we got back.

That evening – much to my surprise – he sent us to our room. I was happy with this but I also felt on edge, as I could never predict what actions he might make. Maybe he was tired from working at the store all day.

Sarah looked at me oddly with an expression that silently asked what she should do, as we found that we didn't know what to do with ourselves. I looked over towards the tea set that had been left, untouched, for some time, and began to imagine that we were back at Nanny and Grandad's house, where we could play and laugh without a care in the world. Oh, how I prayed that we were back at Nanny and Grandad's house!

CHAPTER SIX

FAMILY VISIT

THE NEXT DAY, Mummy told us that Nanny and Grandad would be coming over at the weekend to visit. Had my prayers been answered? Nanny and Grandad were sure to see how we were treated now and would surely say something. Excitement ran through me, and I could feel my face bursting like a sudden ray of sunshine on a cloudy day. This feeling bewildered me, as I very rarely experienced this.

But, of course, that feeling was short-lived – shot down (as fast as it had arisen) by him.

He ordered us into the living room, sniggering that he had questions to ask. Clearly, his nightly entertainment had started again. "Both of you, here! In front of me!" he barked.

I stood in front of the living room window, doing as he ordered.

"Now, who can tell me how many days there are in a year?"

I nervously started thinking of the answer to the question, but I was eight years old and I just had no idea.

"OK, how many weeks are there in a year then?"

I frantically wracked my brains; I truly didn't know and will admit that I did not pay attention at school. I could feel my breathing increasing as the tears started to fill my eyes. Was this a test?

He teased us with delight, revelling in the thought that we were about to earn ourselves another strike. Sarah and I both stared at each other in the hope that one of us knew the answer, but I knew she didn't by the sad look in her eyes and the panic that riddled her face, as if she had just spotted a spider that she wanted me to get rid of.

"No, neither of you know," he said, clearly loving our distress. "Well, I guess you've both earnt yourselves a strike, haven't you? So, what will your punishment be?"

I could see he was taking pleasure in thinking of a punishment for us, and after a few moments he ordered us both down to the ground to do twenty push-ups.

Kneeling on the floor to take up the push-up position, we both looked at each other pitifully. He wanted twenty push-ups, but as I pulled my body up and down, it was hard to keep my body weight lifted.

My hair lingered in and around my face – blurring my vision around me – so when he grabbed me with the full force of his hands, he took me by surprise. He pulled me up from the floor, grunting to himself that my hair was too long and was getting in the way. "Go get me the scissors out of the kitchen!" he ordered, letting go of my hair.

I ran to the kitchen as fast as I could so as not to upset him any further, and then ran back and passed him the scissors.

His pale, overbearing body stood glaring at me from above. Then, roughly, he turned me around and began to cut my thin blonde hair. I stood as cold and as dead as the night while he continued to cut my hair, closing my eyes so I wouldn't sway off balance.

I watched as long strands of my hair fell to the ground, but I didn't care; I just didn't have it in me to spill my tears over having my hair cut – after all, he'd done a lot worse to me. In a minute it would all be over anyway.

"That's better, four eyes. What do you say?"

I turned to look at him in confusion, as I didn't understand what response he wanted.

His face became meaner and angrier as he spat, "Thank you would be nice!"

"Thank you," I replied.

"Thank you what?" he asked with such venom, as if I'd forgotten my place in the world.

"Thank you, sir."

"Go stand over there. Now, your turn, Sarah."

Moving back towards the window, I glanced briefly at Sarah, who was trembling like an aspen leaf and who looked more upset than I did at the thought of having her hair cut.

One by one Sarah's brown curls fell to the floor – her hair was thicker than mine and much prettier – and when he'd finally finished, it was just above her shoulders, like mine.

I hated him. What pleasure did he get out of cutting our hair?

We resumed the push-ups, and when I finally caved in after just a few, I earnt myself another strike. I was now at strike two – having received both within a matter of minutes – and panic set in as I knew I only had one more to go before I received something that was surely going to hurt.

Sarah had more stamina than me and was very good at the push-ups; either that or she wanted to prove that he couldn't beat her down. I, on the other hand, had to stay in the push-up position whilst Sarah was set free from this torment. Every so often he would order me to put my bottom down as I lifted it higher in order to release the strain and aches from my arms. Not wanting to receive my third strike kept me motivated; I couldn't bear any more punishment in one night.

Mummy couldn't come home quick enough; Greg's attention always diverted towards her.

My hair no longer clung to my face as I started to sweat from the torment of trying to stay in one place for a long period of time. I prayed that he'd release me – surely he would when Mummy was home? He wouldn't need me for entertainment then; he'd have Mummy.

Finally, she arrived. "What's happened to Sarah's hair?" she asked timidly, not noticing that I was on the floor in a push-up position, my hair also cut.

"It was getting too long and it needed doing," Greg replied. "Besides, it will stop the nits getting in from school." And with that Mummy agreed, just like that – no other solidarity needed.

How long was he going to keep me like this for? I could feel my eyes swelling as the thought of being here all night ran through me like a lightning bolt. Why did I succumb to tears all the time? My whimpers began and my nose started to stream, adding to my panic as I realised I didn't have any hands free to wipe my tears or my nose. I just couldn't face any more trouble – not tonight.

"Let Kelly get up now, Greg – let's have a nice evening tonight," Mummy said with a hint of persuasion in her tone.

"Right girls, both of you can sit facing the wall tonight," he said as if he was doing us a favour by taking Mummy's side.

As we both sat staring at the same blank monotonous wall, the sounds of the background soon became a distant memory as my legs began to stiffen from sitting in the same position for hours – what I thought to be a less challenging position turned out to be just as hard.

Too scared to move in case he noticed me, which usually prompted him to play one of his cruel games, I would gently ease my legs from under me and sit on one side of my thigh, alternating this every so often once I felt the pins and needles starting. Every nerve in my legs seemed like a strained guitar string, ready to snap with my every move.

After what seemed like hours, just as my eyes were starting to feel incredibly heavy, we were eventually given permission to go to bed. I never said goodnight to either one of them – the only one I would ever say this to was Sarah.

Crawling into bed with Sarah, I was tired and desperate to sleep, and soon I sank into a horrible nightmarish dream.

He had entered our room, his stone-cold eyes and sunken mouth opening widely, as if to laugh hysterically. He held a pair of scissors in one hand, and as his wide mouth opened even more, blood seeped out and trickled down his chin. I ran into the darkness and fell onto my duvet – where the remains of my hair lay – to escape him. Nearer and nearer he came at me, the echo of his laughter haunting the room. 'You can't run from me, child!' he yelled.

I cried myself awake, clutching at my hair and shivering from the sweat of my terror.

Most nights I'd be tired – after feeling like I'd done a hard night's work – but as dawn broke the very next day, I would always find the strength to get ready for school no matter how tired I felt, as this was my time and place of solace.

As the weekend drew closer my thoughts about Nanny and Grandad intensified – they were sure to know what he was doing to us. Greg continued with his foul games of push-ups; he was determined to wear me down even further.

On the Friday evening before Nanny and Grandad were due, he escorted me and Sarah to the bathroom and crouched down to sit on the toilet seat. Then, rounding us up like sheep, he huddled us together in the dark.

Why would he always take us into the bathroom to talk to us? I wondered. The light stayed off, making the bathroom look even dingier than it normally did and leaving my imagination to run wild in the gloom. The light from the hallway gleamed onto certain spots of the wall, spilling shadows of unknown origins that I later established was just a toothbrush. I looked hard to find the source, but it wasn't long before my attention was focused on Greg as he began to warn me and Sarah to be on our best behaviour when the family arrived.

Standing at eye level with Greg, I stared at him curiously, noticing that his glasses amplified his cold, dark eyes; it looked like I was staring at him through a magnifying glass. Did he know this? I wondered. Was that why he called me four eyes, because he in fact saw double of everything?

I stood clinging onto his every word as if it would be the end of me if I didn't, nodding furiously so he knew I understood his every question – because if I didn't, the penalty would fall upon me like a raging thunderstorm.

"Now, Kelly and Sarah, you know what you have to do, don't you?" he asked sternly, leaning in towards us and turning his head slightly to one side as though he was hard of hearing.

"Yes sir," we replied in harmony.

"What's that then?"

Without hesitation we both replied, "Stay quiet and don't say a word unless spoken to, sir."

"That's right, because you don't want me to embarrass you by having to pull your pants down in front of everyone and smacking you, do you?"

Would he really do that? I wondered to myself. Maybe, if he was suggesting that he'd pull our pants down in front of everyone, this was all normal. I didn't want to be embarrassed –especially in front of Nanny and Grandad – and I certainly didn't want them to think I was bad.

He eventually gave us permission to leave the bathroom and return to our bedroom, and once we were back I sat with Sarah, contemplating the words that he'd drilled into us about our behaviour. I had come to the realisation that I couldn't say anything. He would know – he knew everything – and it would be me and Sarah who'd be left with him, not Nanny and Grandad.

As the evening fell upon us, Mummy entered our room and wandered over to the cupboards, her eyes empty and glazed. The most fearful silence grew between us. She jerked her head to look at me and I stared sharply back at her, her eyes so dark and deep they almost cast a shadow. I wondered what she was doing, as she opened the cupboard to pull out two of our best dresses to wear for tomorrow.

"Now girls, when you wake in the morning put these dresses on, as Nanny will be here early."

"Yes Mummy," I replied, hoping that she would come to settle us into bed and give us a goodnight kiss. But she didn't. She simply wandered back out of our room as quickly as she'd entered, leaving silence in her wake. Silence was no longer alien to us; we had soon learnt to only talk when spoken to.

We had forgotten how to play, even when we were kicked out of the house for hours on end. We would often find ourselves sitting on the doorstep through not knowing what to do, having exhausted our play in the park. I hardly noticed George in the house anymore, as Greg was careful to keep him from view of how mean he was to us. It seemed that Sarah and I took too much of his time up, though it was through his own choice. All these thoughts were running through my mind as I retired to bed early.

The following morning my excitement had faded, the remnants of Greg's voice and words sticking at the forefront of my mind.

"Come on Kelly, get dressed," Sarah said with enthusiasm. "Nanny and Grandad are coming!"

For the first time in a long while I could see a sparkle in her eyes; she was just so excited, regardless of what he'd said to us. I didn't want to dampen her mood, even though I'd given up hope of anyone ever knowing what was happening to us – it wasn't right for me to take what little happiness she had away.

I continued to dress while Sarah fixed her hair the best she could, despite having had it cut. It didn't seem to faze her that she had short straggly bits that hung down around her face, which wouldn't quite fix up into her ponytail. I, on the other hand, felt a lot of resentment, and I wasn't even going to attempt to fix my hair – I gave it a quick brush and that was it.

Approaching the kitchen for breakfast, I looked at Mummy and Greg to find that they'd dressed up. No amount of dressing up will hide the person you really are, I thought, as I continued to the table to eat my cornflakes. I was getting older and often found myself thinking horrible, nasty things on a regular occurrence. Was this normal? I'd started to become envious of others and on occasion that even included my own brother and sister.

Mummy was flouncing around the house, her eyes bolting noisily about the room as she straightened the cushions on the chair and gave the coffee table one last wipe with the cloth. I hadn't seen Mummy this nervous in a long time; it was strange to me. She so caringly took the time and the effort to ensure everything was OK for Nanny and Grandad's arrival, yet she didn't run around like this for me and Sarah. She barely did anything for us.

"They're here!" Mummy said with apprehension as she glanced over at Greg, awaiting his approval to answer the door.

My hard-fixed eyes were gazing upon Mummy, so much so that I hardly even noticed him standing at the table.

Thump! The table moved, making me jump almost out of my skin. My eyes squinted, readying myself for a slap that never came. Slowly, I opened my eyes again and looked at Greg, just as he slammed his hands down on the table again. Leaning over, he gave us a hard, cold look, his eyes flashing – a warning, and reminder, of the conversation we'd had the night before.

Finally, after what felt like forever, Greg went and opened the door.

"Hello, Kelly and Sarah!" Nanny said with open arms as she greeted us. She was exactly the same as I remembered her, so caring and attentive with a smile that warmed your heart.

"Hello," I said, cautiously aware that Greg was watching my every move.

The afternoon came too quickly. We'd sat at the kitchen table most of the morning, whilst the grown-ups talked in the living room. We'd found ourselves sitting in silence, listening intently to the conversation that was being had.

Auntie Caroline was due to get married. She had met a wonderful man and his name was Graham and he was going to be my uncle. I heard Nanny describe Auntie Caroline's accomplishments with laughter, all smiles as she went on to explain that she wanted me and Sarah to be bridesmaids at her wedding and that this wedding would be taking place very soon.

I became more and more excited as I continued to sit quietly at the kitchen table, the excitement bubbling up inside me, trying to find a way to escape. I was always aware, however, that Greg was listening and watching, making his presence known as, on occasion, he strutted back and forth to the kitchen.

I sat pondering the dress I would wear to the wedding, with matching shoes that would only complement the dress further. I had never been asked to be a bridesmaid before and I thought I might never be asked again, yet I could still dream of the cakes and treats I would get to eat all day long. I may not have any fairy tale story of my own, I thought, but at least I'd get to be part of someone else's.

The time soon arrived when we were told to go to our rooms. Aware that we had sat for a long period of time in the kitchen, we retired to our room and sat together at the edge of our bed, our hands restlessly clasped together in our laps, waiting for further instructions.

I eventually placed my arm around Sarah and looked at her closely – she looked so much like Daddy. A vision flashed through my mind of Daddy in his white uniform, proud to serve the army men with his curled hair that fought its way out from under his cap. Sarah's curls had now been stripped from her by Greg.

My eyes widened as Mummy opened the bedroom door. The night had slowly crept in and Mummy announced that Nanny and Grandad had gone, and that it was time for bed.

I wanted to protest that we'd been sitting for hours and that we were hungry and thirsty, but I didn't. Languidly, I did as she directed, putting myself to bed full of disappointment that I hadn't been given the chance to say my goodbyes. Was she that ashamed of us that we had to be tucked away like this? Greg had won again. The feeling of defeat ripped through me, the uncertainty of what was to become of us aching inside me. Oh, how I missed Nanny and Grandad's love and gentleness!

I lay curled up in my duvet, the edge of the pillow in one hand and my thumb in the other and drifted off. I was soon woken, however, by footsteps walking across our room.

Peeping from beneath my duvet, my eyes bulged at

him. He was standing there at our window with binoculars again, looking out onto the square. What was he looking at? I didn't care much; I just didn't want him to disturb me and Sarah. Did he know we could see him?

I started to tremble beneath the covers, my mind thinking over all the appalling threats he'd ever given us and wondering which one he'd apply to me if he suspected I was awake.

Rather cowardly, I waited for him to leave, my body aching from trying to keep so still – every itch intensified as I tried so hard not to move. Keeping my eyes shut tight, I waited longingly to hear his footsteps walking back out of the room.

Eventually he left, allowing me to finally move my body. It had become so stiff.

"What was he doing?" Sarah whispered, frightening me. My thoughts were still running scarily wild, not having been given the chance to disappear.

"I don't know what he was doing, but he comes in quite a lot," I replied. "I didn't realise you were still awake."

"I wasn't – he woke me. I always know when he's in our room."

I never understood why he did what he did. Why he came in our room, why he liked to see us in pain… none of it.

Before I knew it, morning had arrived. It was

Sunday and Mummy and Greg would both be at home today. I got up to get dressed and then hurried to the kitchen to get some breakfast. I was famished and could have eaten a horse.

Greg was sprawled out on the couch in his unwelcoming brown shorts.

"Sir, can I get some breakfast please?" I asked sheepishly, hoping he wouldn't deny me considering I'd had no dinner last night.

"Yes but hurry up – I have plans for you and your sister today."

Those words stole the hunger straight from my stomach, but I continued to walk to the kitchen, nervously shutting the door behind me in the hope of shutting him out.

After fixing my breakfast – which I planned to eat as slowly as I could, to prolong his plans as much as possible – I stared at the telephone beside the kitchen table, longing to be brave enough to pick it up, just once, to call for help. But the potential consequences always got the better of me.

As I sat there munching on my cornflakes, Greg approached the table. "What's taking you so long?" he scorned.

Was he not tired of this? I wondered. Because I sure was. "I'm finished, sir," I said, leaving the rest to be thrown away, so as not to anger him any further.

"Right, come here," he ordered, before calling Sarah over too. "Now, who can tell me how many days there are in a year?"

Not this again, I thought to myself. Why hadn't I found out this information when I was at school? "I don't know, sir," I bravely responded. I really didn't know, and I hoped that by being honest he would be gentle with his punishment.

He stared at me in horror and disappointment, as if I should have known the answer by now. I could tell by his look that this was going to be bad. I had failed me and Sarah again. "I want twenty push-ups now, on the spot!" he ordered.

As I crouched down on all fours to start my push-ups, Sarah knelt beside me. She was much better at this than me; she had the strength, while I clearly didn't.

My eyes watered at the thought of the day ahead as I began to count my push-ups. Somehow, I managed to do the twenty, and then I waited for him to order us both to stand.

"Good," he praised. "Now, again – how many days are there in a year?"

Was this going to continue all throughout the day? I wondered. I sincerely hoped not, as I really didn't know the answer. I hung my head in shame rather than answering, and he knew I didn't have an answer for him.

"Give me twenty."

Again, I resumed the push-up position and started to count. I already felt defeated, and he knew it. It was the perfect opportunity for him to punish me further.

My attempts to push up and down soon became slower and more feeble. I could feel his eyes watching me, piercing right through me like rays of the sun burning pale skin. He had summoned my eyes to swell once again. I just couldn't help it; the thought of having to do this all day tore through me as quickly as a volcano rips through a mountain.

"I can't do this!" I spluttered.

"There is no such word as 'can't'!" he shot back. "Now finish this before I give you more to do!"

Sarah was already waiting for permission to be released, and in that moment, I felt like such a burden – now I was the cause of Sarah's continuing state of pain.

"Greg, what's going on?" I heard my mummy say then. "It's Sunday – surely the girls don't need to be doing this today?" she asked cowardly. The sound of Mummy's voice no longer comforted me; I did not see her as my saviour.

"Are you challenging me, Lindy?" he asked.

He rose from his seated position, ordering me and Sarah to stand to one side while he moved the furniture to clear a space on the floor. I glanced at

Mummy – she looked pitiful, unhappy, her face lowering into her hair as she pondered the decision she had to make.

I, on the other hand, was grateful that I'd been released from my position, though I was unsure about what was going to happen next. My thoughts came to me as snide unwanted conceptions, bringing about hatred that wished to lurk in my mind, to make me continuously miserable. It was hard to drive my own thoughts away because I no longer knew how I felt about Mummy – though I knew I hated him!

Mummy wasn't even dressed – she still wore her nighty. Did he expect her to fight like that?

But she did.

Slowly, she walked towards him, her timid, shy voice trying to express how ridiculous this was at this time of the morning.

He didn't care. Crouching down to the floor, he positioned his arms out in front of him, reaching out to her as though he was greeting her.

I felt a little relief as I stood watching Mummy creep towards to him. The relief I felt at not having to do the push-ups any longer, however, didn't last long. I just hoped Mummy would do a good job in beating him down so I wouldn't have to take over. At first it was hard watching Mummy fight him, but as the years went on, I no longer feared for Mummy, as she certainly didn't fear for me!

The punches Mummy threw were with love and passion, though she didn't stand a chance against him if he really wanted to hurt her.

I stood and listened as he wrestled her to the ground; I couldn't tolerate watching the whole thing through, so I would pull my head down towards my chin and stare at the carpet, counting as far as I could in my head. Whenever I lost track, I would start all over again.

CHAPTER SEVEN

DADDY'S LETTER

THE FOLLOWING MORNING, it was time to get back to school. The weekend had ended, and at least I would have a few hours of peace away from him.

When school started to come to an end, however, my panic seemed to switch on, just like clockwork; an hour before I knew the bell was going to ring, I would start dreading the thought of having to go home.

On this day, unknown to Sarah and me, Daddy had written us a letter. Greg must have arrived home early or not attended work, as when we walked into the living room, he held up a piece of paper in his hand, scowling at us – and clearly expecting us to know what it was that he was holding.

"Do you know what I have here?"

"No sir," I replied, having no idea what he was talking about.

"It's a letter from your father," Greg explained. "Apparently, he hasn't received a phone call from you recently and is wondering why, so tell me: when have you been calling your father?"

Oh no. My panic intensified as I realised I'd been caught, my legs turning to jelly as I felt what seemed to be an electric shock run through my whole body, making it shake uncontrollably. I knew that I didn't need to speak, that my body spoke a thousand words, yet he wanted a response. "I've called him a few times at the phone box, sir," I said. I knew I couldn't lie and that I had to be frank about it, even though I was blubbering in my response as the tears ran down my face. I wasn't sorry for calling Daddy, just sorry that Daddy hadn't listened, instead leaving me and Sarah alone with this terrible man.

His cold stare pierced through me as he stood watching me and Sarah, and the two of us clasped our hands together for comfort, knowing this was going to be bad. I could never tell whether his long, fixed, vacant look was because he was thinking up a punishment, or because he'd already thought one up and couldn't wait to inflict it upon us.

Moving slowly towards us, he ripped the letter

in half and handed us both a piece. "Take this, fold the piece of paper up into a square, and follow me."

"Yes sir," I replied after a slight hesitation, looking at Sarah vacantly and hoping she'd have some idea of what was about to happen. Her confused expression told me otherwise.

He walked back towards the sofa and told us both to sit in front of the window on our knees, facing him. I cautiously yet promptly did as I was told, my mind running a thousand miles an hour thinking of all the possible punishments we were going to receive for Daddy writing to us.

We weren't even going to get the chance to read his letter, so I would have no idea what Daddy had said to us.

As I placed myself down onto my knees and held my daddy's letter in my hand, I couldn't bear to look at Greg.

"Now, four eyes," he said, "I want you to place this letter in your mouth and hold it there, but be careful not to touch it with your tongue or to get it wet, because if you do then you will have earnt yourself a strike." He then proceeded to explain that we were both to hold this letter for a week in our mouths and could only take it out to eat, drink, sleep, and go to school.

Slowly, I did as I was told and placed my daddy's

letter in my mouth, promptly stopping my tears from rolling down my face with the sleeve of my jumper so as not to get my letter wet. Sarah did the same, sitting beside me and placing her half of the letter inside her own mouth.

At this point I didn't know where to look, though I thought the punishment wasn't too bad; at least I wasn't in any pain with this one, and all I had to do was ensure I didn't get the letter wet. I fixed my gaze on everything around me apart from him. The whispers of his brown shorts, the sound of his voice, the heavy tread of his bare feet, the sight of his face, with his glasses enlarging his pale stone-cold evil eyes... I just couldn't face it. To look at him was to loathe him.

I sat there, wondering how long it would be before Mummy came home from work. Surely, she would think this ridiculous, holding a letter in our mouths.

I had nothing better to do than watch as George played with his cars across the table. He reached out to us on a couple of occasions with a car in his hand, to suggest that we play with him. Every time I caught a glimpse of his look, I would quickly place my gaze onto the floor, so as not to give him false hope that I would come and play. Oh, how I would give anything to play with him right now, rather than feeling like a pair of dogs, sitting to attention, waiting for our next commands!

Eventually Mummy arrived, faltering by the living room door with her bags of shopping.

Slowly lifting my eyes bravely towards Mummy, I waited for her to look back. I didn't want to plead with my eyes, yet I did; I begged for help, for her to come to our defence and to tell him to stop right now!

Then, with a quick glance my way, her cold and scornful eyes lowered, turning back to the shopping in her hands as she continued through to the kitchen.

We would never win her over, and he always came first for her – it was like we didn't exist. My breathing was loud, my heart became hollow, and the ache in my chest reached right down to my bare feet. I felt my whimpers go unheard again.

Greg eventually allowed us to take the piece of paper from our mouths. It was no longer Daddy's letter; it was just a bittersweet reminder that we would never get to speak to Daddy again.

Carefully, I removed the paper from my mouth, knowing it was wet. The secretions in my mouth had softened it up, in amongst my tearful pleas to Mummy when she'd returned.

After carrying out an inspection Greg shook his head in disapproval, and then – with a slight curved smile – he took his eyes from the paper and focused them on mine. "It looks like you've earnt yourself another strike, Kelly," he said coldly, "but your mother says its dinner time now, so I will think of a suitable punishment after."

I sat at the table, silent. I couldn't eat for fear of what awaited me after. I just picked at my food, eating a few forkfuls and moving the rest around on my plate.

Sarah and I didn't speak. There were no words that could comfort us, as we both knew the punishment would be bad. It was always bad. Instead we would give each other the odd glance and a slight smile, letting each other know that it was me and her against the world.

I could always sense his presence; he was like a bad smell, lingering in the room for hours and hours.

"Both of you get up and clean this kitchen," Greg said suddenly. "I'm going to time you – let's say fifteen minutes, and your time starts… now!" He was ridiculing us, bringing his wrist – where his watch rested – close to his eyes.

I jumped up from the table in a panic, clearing the plates and then starting to wash the pots. I had no way of checking the time and so had no idea how much time we had left to finish cleaning the kitchen. Still, we did our best to try and work as a team. I washed the pots and Sarah put them away, while trying to clean the sides as well.

Then, without warning, he shouted from the living room, "Time's up, get here!"

We stood like soldiers in front of the sofa, waiting for his response as he sighed loudly while inspecting our work in the kitchen. I knew we had failed. He knew we had failed. I stared aimlessly at Mummy, who never turned towards us, again begging silently for her to step in. She never did.

He emerged from the kitchen to give me my second strike and Sarah her first. "Now, let's try this again, shall we? You have ten minutes to finish that kitchen off."

"Yes sir," we replied.

My body began to shake. I looked at Sarah to let her know that I was one strike away from my third and that I couldn't afford to get another one. The nervousness of being on strike two was the most awful feeling, and my shaking body prevented me from wanting to move.

"Come on, Kelly!" Sarah screeched, her voice imploring me to move, fearing that I would reach my third strike.

It hardly seemed any time at all before we were called back into the living room. I had reached my third strike, having received all three in just one afternoon.

"What am I going to do with you, Kelly?" he mocked, as if I was supposed to answer his question. "Well?" he sneered.

"I don't know, sir." By now I was wailing and

shaking, clasping my troubled hands together in front of me, nervously awaiting my punishment.

He started to move the furniture away from the centre of the room, and I furiously scanned the living room and out to the hallway, but Mummy was nowhere to be seen. I detested these fights of his – I saw no purpose in them other than to make me suffer.

Greg carefully placed himself down onto the living room floor and ordered me over. With every step I took towards him, it felt like my legs were stuck in quicksand. I was jittery, shrinking with each stride. My hands clenched to feeble fists and my face was overrun by my tears.

I was already defeated; as I endeavoured to punch him, it turned into me simply punching thin air. My half-hearted attempt caught his eye though, and his face turned to anger.

"What's wrong with you, do you not want to fight me?" he asked.

My silence seemed to crash to earth, like a chandelier that had fallen and shattered into a million pieces. Then, to my horror, he seized my throat and scowled at me, slowly tightening his grip.

I coughed, forcing him to release his grip from around my throat, and then he started to laugh, seemingly amused. It was then that he started daring me to go and get a knife.

"I know you want to, just go and grab a sharp knife and stab me with it – I dare you!"

I wanted to – boy, did I want to – but I was old enough to know it would be fateful, more so for me than for him.

He continued to persist that I get this knife while every bone in my body froze where I stood, my impulse telling me not to move even though he continued to scowl at me.

Suddenly, I was scared. Really scared. Scared that I was going to die.

I glanced at Sarah to look for answers that weren't there, then I closed my eyes to try and shut out this man's voice – out of sight, out of mind – only to hear my chest fluttering away erratically instead. Was he being serious?

Then, finally, Mummy stepped in. "Enough, Greg, please," she said weakly.

Was she finally scared that I might get hurt? Or was she scared that he might get hurt? Either way, her glowing eyes betrayed my love, not looking at me once. I wondered what his sadistic mind was thinking – was he contemplating whether he should take Mummy's advice?

I continued to stand nervously before him, secretly praying that he would stop this and send us to bed. To whom I was praying, though, I still wasn't sure.

"Your mother wins this time, now get out of my sight, the both of you!" he growled.

Without a second thought, I turned my back on him and scarpered to my room before he changed his mind.

Into my dreams crept this dark, scary monstrous being resembling Greg. He stole into my night. With my eyes firmly shut closed, he thought I was asleep as he approached with a knife. I screamed as he hung over me with his bulging eyes staring wildly into mine, one hand placed on my chest and the other holding a shiny silver knife. No one could hear my screams but Greg, who placed his hand over my mouth, burying my scream back into my dream.

I tossed and writhed, trying to escape this monstrosity, awaking Sarah as I wrestled with the duvet.

"Kelly, wake up, it's just a dream!" Sarah uttered as quickly as she could so I wouldn't wake anyone up.

It hadn't felt like a dream – more like a nightmare!

"What was it about?" she asked in concern.

Not wanting to worry her, I decided to keep it to myself. My nightmare had frightened me, so it was sure to frighten her if I told her about it. "It was nothing," I told her. "I'm OK, now go back to sleep and don't worry."

Placing my head back on the pillow, I placed my thumb in my mouth and closed my eyes. The dream felt so real that not even the comfort of my own thumb would settle my restless mind. I continued to toss and turn, hoping the bedroom door wouldn't open. The last thing I wanted now was for him to appear.

I never really remembered my dreams, and so assumed that I probably didn't dream. After all, there was nothing to dream of – there was no happiness, nothing to look forward to, and my daily routine pretty much consisted of the same things, day in and day out. The memory of the nightmare stayed with me until morning, and as I got ready for school, I felt weak; I couldn't get to school fast enough.

The day had passed as quick as it had sprung, and I knew that when I returned home, I would have to hold Daddy's letter in my mouth yet again. With every ounce of hope I had left, I hoped Greg had forgotten that Daddy had written to us.

But when I returned the two pieces of the letter were there, laid neatly on the table, ready for us to pick up.

This time, though, we were allowed to sit on the chair, rather than sit on the floor – probably so he didn't have to look at us. Although, perhaps this was because he didn't want to be reminded of what evil he held, which he would be if we sat in front of him.

I sat in the chair with Sarah beside me, putting

the letter in my mouth and trying to let my mind wander to the television. After all, it was on and we rarely got to watch it. I soon realised, however, that it took deep concentration to ensure that I didn't get the letter wet – especially after remembering the consequences I'd suffered the night before.

The hours crawled by like years. Every minute we sat in his impalpable presence was with terrible unease, being as still as possible like a pair of frozen statues so that we weren't being too obvious with our existence.

This was soon to change, however, as we couldn't help but get the letter wet. I was on my first strike, but Sarah had already reached her third. It was an impossible task that he'd set, and I imagined that the letter would have disintegrated by the time the end of the week neared. Though perhaps that was his plan, to give him a feasible excuse as to why we never got to read it?

After he'd ordered us to get up, we both stood side by side, waiting for our fate. I really didn't want to bear witness to what was about to happen to Sarah, yet I had no choice – I was sure he relished in the fact that we both had to watch each other's punishment.

His empty eyes spread out over the living room as he misplaced the furniture. I was then ordered to stand to one side while he summoned Sarah to approach him for a fight. He was now on her level, coaxing her forward.

My desolate eyes wilted around the room, until I eventually closed them in an attempt to shut out his hateful voice. Sarah was not being her usual self. I could tell by her lack of emotion, her laboured breathing as she tried to punch. She would usually be fierce and full of strength, but not today.

I couldn't help but stare in shock and disbelief when he told Sarah to go and get a knife. I was angry, wanting to scream at her, 'No, don't do it, it's a trap!' His game hadn't worked with me so now he was trying it on with Sarah. Mummy wasn't here to help or to tell him that was enough this time, so it had to be me who had to step up and face my fear.

Quickly I brushed away my tears, before I faced him and yelled, in a small, faltering voice, "No!"

What had I done?

Kneeling up from his position, he threw me a scornful glance, displeasing to the eye. After a few moments he was facing me fully, glaring down on me and forcing me to hang my head in shame. Listening to Sarah's choking sobs and cries, he placed his hand under my chin, forcefully pushing my face up to greet his. Then, with his other monstrous hand he struck me immediately across my face, causing me to lose my standing posture and fall to the ground.

Sarah continued to weep uncontrollably, memories of the past looming up from when he'd burnt her hand for doing such a thing. I felt so bad for her.

Walking away from my fallen position, his chilling body worked his way into the kitchen. I took the opportunity to glance at Sarah, shaking my head vigorously whilst placing a finger to my mouth, signalling for her to be quiet. My motions and anguish finally reached her; she understood and nodded back, attempting to dry away the tears before his return.

Standing by the door, I noticed that he raised his head high to watch our reactions as he pulled out a knife – the knife he had willingly ordered both of us to get.

My thoughts yapped around me frantically. I was sure this was it – that today, within minutes, one of us was going to end up dead, and there was no one and no way to stop him.

I swallowed heavily, the same thoughts as always running through my mind – to run, to run far away – but self-doubt stopped me in my tracks. As I stood there, trembling, I felt this unwanted pull to stay. At least I knew this house, this man. Outside, the big wide world was unknown to me. I feared that too.

Greg played with the knife, slapping the sharp shiny bit from one hand to the other while we both stared at him in a daze, like little lost puppies looking confused and helpless.

"Do you know how to handle a knife, and the right way to carry one?" he asked us.

Was this another one of his games? My anxiety heightened as I answered his question. "No sir," I replied, fighting back the tears to lessen his anger.

"Come here and I will show you."

I hovered near to him, every bone in my body trying to trust him, though I was quivering with the suspicious fear that my life was about to my end.

To my disbelief he handed me the knife handle, whilst he held the sharp end. Continuing to hold the knife with a firm grip, I tried to take it from him, but he pulled me closer to him, placing the knife against his belly.

"Go on then, I know you want to," he growled, insinuating that I wanted to stab him.

With every inch of my body, I wanted to. I was engulfed with confusion. If only my secret thoughts could be heard, yet every withering ounce of emotion I had left in me was telling me not to say it, not to do it. Alarmed, I cried out, "No, I love you!" to save my own skin.

Somehow, I knew I would not win this fight, giving him the opportunity to fill Mummy's head with all sorts of cowardly lies as I lay dying in the hospital. I pictured it: one less mouth to feed, one less child to clothe, one less child to hear. Besides, why wait till I was sixteen to get rid of me, if it could be done now?

Rather cowardly, I dropped my end of the knife, hoping that my words would end this whole thing. My deceitful words would leave a scar – much like Sarah's scar – that I would have to bear for the rest of my life, for I sure didn't mean what I'd said.

Once he'd realised I wasn't falling for his trickery, he turned to Sarah. "What about you, Sarah? Do you fancy having a go?"

It didn't take much today for Sarah to break down crying. She was normally the stronger one of the two of us, and I often envied her for that, but today she was just broken. Was it the thought of never getting to read Daddy's letter? I wondered. I hadn't given much thought to asking her about it.

"No sir." She turned her face away so she wouldn't have to look at his disappointment.

As he turned abruptly to place the knife on the kitchen table, Greg's overbearing existence felt even more chilling. I stood motionless, never moving until I was ordered to do so.

"Both of you, stand over at the wall on your tip-toes, nose touching… you know the drill."

Quickly and swiftly, we both went and stood in front of the plain boring wall, Sarah giving one last wipe of her face to dry away the tears before we took up our positions.

I hated this position with a vengeance. I found myself wanting to drift off to sleep, having counted every mark visible to the naked eye from where I stood. I would give anything right now for the wall to be painted a different colour, just to give me something else to stare at. The burning sensation that ripped through my calves as I stood for hours on tiptoe tortured my soul, one half of me wanting to place my heels to the floor and the other half shouting, 'No, don't do it!'

I knew that Sarah felt the same; she must have done because if I could feel the anguishing pain in my calves then she surely did too.

I would count down the minutes until I'd be set free, over and over in my head – having nothing else better to do – until I heard Mummy's voice. It would only be a matter of time before she pleaded with him to let us go to bed. I never knew how long it would take her, but she had to get him to release us, as we both had school the next day.

CHAPTER EIGHT

CAROLINE'S WEDDING

SCHOOL. WHEN I stood thinking about it, I came to realise that school often astonished me. I would hear how my fellow school friends hated being there and would never quite know what to say in response. I loved being there. I thanked God for school. Each day when I got to school, I knew Greg was far away from me; he couldn't touch me, and I couldn't earn my strikes there. Unlike everyone else who saw the weekend as their saviour, school was my heaven and evenings and weekends were my hell, where a captor awaited my return. These thoughts, vivid in my mind, played over and over again like a broken record. I couldn't wait now until I turned sixteen, so I could rid myself from this horrid place.

It was soon announced to us that we would indeed be attending Auntie Caroline's wedding. Finally, something to look forward to, where I would be around my true family – those that actually cared for me and Sarah. By now I no longer played with my mixed emotions; I knew that I couldn't let anyone know what was going on at home. So, I would remain quiet and be accepting of my fate.

I managed to smile when we both put on our matching bridesmaid dresses, which had been carefully picked out by Auntie Caroline. Mine was a white dress that was broken up with pale blue spots, covering the entire dress. Sarah's was the same but in pale pink. Ribbons were tied around our waists, complemented by big bows that reached down to our ankles, with plain shiny white shoes to match. I felt so grown up – almost like royalty – as a French braid was put in my hair to complete the look.

Nanny's house was full of laughter and joy. Everyone was scarpering about in the midst of all the chaos, trying to get everything ready for Caroline's big day. For a brief moment, my troubles were forgotten.

I observed all the children that were being fussed over by their mothers and their aunts – having their hair tied with bows and adjusted, the boys having their suits and ties straightened in readiness to enter the church.

"You both look beautiful," Auntie Caroline told us. Smiling intently, she was clearly pleased that everything was going to plan.

I knew in that moment that I definitely couldn't say anything; I didn't want to ruin her big day, and everyone was just so busy that no one would have the time to sit down and listen to my story anyway.

The arrangements of the flowers on the tables and in our hair were all matching, the flowers in my hair running all the way down to the very end of my braid – blue flowers for me and pink for Sarah. I felt so pretty. I drank in the moment of happiness, as I imagined I would never again feel this way. My home was the opposite to laughter, smiles, and enjoyment; instead it was full of despair, torment, and heartache. I had to make myself over and become happy, learn how to smile again – never frown – and become cheerful like Sarah.

On the grounds of the church several cars were parked, one completely attired with twisted coils and a big bow, ready to take the bride and groom away. My eyes lit up to a joyful mixture of light blue and pink balloons, that had been carefully placed around the bannisters.

When everyone was inside the church and seated,

the bridal chorus began. All heads turned to face the back of the church, all eyes on the bride as Grandad took her left arm and started walking her down the aisle.

I was walking behind Caroline, and as I made my way down the aisle of the church I was in awe – I could never have pictured something like this ever happening to me. Her long white dress that trailed on the floor behind was stunning; embroidery covered the whole dress along with a two tier veil, and she had white roses embedded in the front of her hair, matching her bridesmaids. She carried a rose silk bouquet as she continued towards the pastor, where she was met by Uncle Graham, her husband-to-be.

Graham looked handsome dressed in his army uniform, wearing a red beret on his head and with a medal attached to his jacket, though by now I loathed anyone from the army. I imagined them all to be like Greg – full of orders and obedience to others that lived by these three strikes. But not Uncle Graham: he had a side to him that was caring and loving, and he probably wouldn't hurt a fly. He was full of small talk and laughter – unlike Greg, who never seemed to laugh but always stood to attention. He would scowl at people with an unease about him, to let it be known that he himself despised all people apart from Mummy.

Uncle Graham was frozen where he stood, looking taller than usual and with more confidence as his bride walked over to him.

The music came to a stop and the room filled with silence. Then there was the exchanging of the vows, so formal yet so endearing.

"Dearly beloved, we gather here today to witness this man and woman joining together in holy matrimony."

Excitedly, with trembling fingers, Graham placed the ring on Caroline's finger.

And then, finally, the pastor – his voice now raised with passion – declared, "You may now kiss the bride."

I watched Auntie Caroline and Uncle Graham share a sweet kiss, and if I wasn't mistaken, I was sure I saw tears fill her eyes as she did so.

As I watched the happy couple, I thought to myself that maybe – one day, when I had rid myself of Greg – I could buy myself any dress I desired.

Soon enough, the day came to an end, and I knew I would have to slip out of my dress, changing from this princess I had become back to reality – that of a girl with straggly hair, who never dreamed of placing flowers in it.

I didn't want to leave, my heart pulling as I watched Mummy say her goodbyes. Every muscle in my chest screamed, wanted to beg her not to let us go and to let us stay with Nanny and Grandad instead, but I couldn't due to the sheer fear of Greg's reaction. I feared that this left my face pale and withdrawn as I felt the deep sickness from the pit of my stomach arise slowly and surely within me.

Once we reached home, we were both sent to bed. It was late, and I was thankful that, for once, we were allowed to end the day with no forms of punishment. Yet when my head hit the pillow, the anxiety of the weekend not being over hit me hard in my chest. There was no school tomorrow, so I didn't know what would become of us.

I was the first awake. I glanced to Sarah next to me, still sound asleep. The sun beamed in quite brightly through my bedroom window and as I listened attentively, there was silence. I couldn't hear George or Mummy and so assumed that everyone was still asleep.

I climbed out of bed to look through my bedroom window at the square, where I saw Greg opening the off-licence store. A burst of happiness ran through me – if he was working today, then that meant he wouldn't be home and I could relax for once. I scattered to get dressed and ran through the motions of getting my own breakfast without the fear of him walking in at any moment. I loved days like this.

Upon entering the kitchen, I saw that Mummy was there, washing the dishes. "Morning, Mummy," I said brightly, "can I make some breakfast?"

"Yes, and when you're done with your breakfast, Greg wants you down in the shop to help him for the day."

No! I screamed to myself. Why would he need me today? "I don't want to help him today, Mummy; I would rather stay here with you," I pleaded pitifully in the hope that she would actually listen for once and allow me to stay home. But who was I kidding? She did as she was told. She never stood up to him, only in desperate times of need.

I bowed my head and continued to get my breakfast, drawing out the time it took me to eat; I wanted to ensure that I spent every minute I could at home.

"Where are you going?" Sarah asked, appearing from our bedroom and watching while I put my coat on.

"I have to go and help Greg for the day," I said sadly, even though I knew she couldn't help me in any way.

I left the house and continued over to the front door of the off-licence. Entering the store, I immediately felt his presence; it was always so cold and stifling. I wondered if anyone else felt this or whether it was just me.

"Get to the back and start by breaking up the boxes ready for rubbish."

"Yes sir."

I never took my time when I was given an order; I would always hurry, like my life depended on it.

The back of the store was cold, covered in big grey bricks that gave the room an uneasy atmosphere. It was an unwelcoming feeling, not helped by the lack of decoration or furniture – there were just empty boxes and stacks of beer cans and bottles. At the end of the room was a wooden door that led out onto a yard filled with dumpsters, where the rubbish would go.

I began to lift the empty boxes, which I would tear apart and crush down with my feet, one by one till I had a stack of them. I worked tirelessly for him, so that I wouldn't have to endure any of his punishment when we got home. I wanted him to see that I could work hard and that he didn't have to give me any orders.

I would then pick up as many stacked boxes as I could and haul them over to the bins outside. I didn't ask for a thing, not even help.

After a while it was time to make my way home for teatime. Oh, how I couldn't wait to get back and relax after all the straining I'd done, lifting the boxes into the bin.

Upon reaching home, I realised how famished

I was – all that work had made me build up a real appetite. When I walked into the kitchen, however, I was presented with a meal I hated: chilli con carne, containing the curry powder I disliked intensely.

I picked at the food, trying to separate the rice from the meat and only eating around the edges of the bowl. I couldn't understand why it had to be so hot, leaving the roof of my mouth burnt. My tongue swelled so that I could scarcely taste the actual meal. Greg liked it this way, but I certainly didn't.

The first thing he did when he entered was to look at my plate; he stood there, cruelly staring right at me and then back at my plate. He hadn't even taken off his coat or shoes – he too must have been hungry – and his deliberate lingering made me conscious that he didn't like me picking at my food.

He turned and walked towards the spice cupboard, and I dreaded what was coming next.

I was right: he paced right back to me at the table where I sat, and as I gazed down at my plate he grabbed a spoon, scooped up some chilli powder, and told me to open my mouth. I looked at him to give him one last plea with my eyes, mutely expressing that I didn't want to. "I said open!" he repeated with hate in his tone, and I didn't dare disobey him.

Reluctantly I opened my mouth, allowing him to place the hot chilli powder inside. I closed my burning eyes once the chilli powder had touched my tongue – to stop the tears from rolling down my face – while I tried to swallow the spice. The awful taste surrounded my mouth. My throat tightened, my mouth now so dry I quivered at the sight of the water on the table. I could feel my already hot cheeks flush with warmth as I reached up with both hands to support the weight of my head with every swallow.

I regretted not eating my dinner; it would have been less painful to have done so. My tears streamed down my cheeks like a waterfall, and with his eagerness not satisfied with just one mouthful of chilli powder, he then shoved in a second.

I started to cough, heaving and spluttering bits of wet chilli powder from my mouth, which only angered him further. I was sure that I was choking. My throat felt like it was closing, defying me to swallow any more.

By now I was overwhelmed with the amount of saliva that had increased in my mouth, and with the chilli powder that had overridden all the cracks within it. I heaved once more in desperation to spit out the contents as he overshadowed me with his presence.

But this was not to be, so bit by bit I forced myself to swallow what was left in my mouth. I looked up in misery as he left my side, content with the outcome he had achieved. I glanced at Mummy who returned to the kitchen, sending us both to bed again with hardly a glance back at me, unloved and untouched.

The hours dragged by like years.

I was barely eleven years old now, and I kept finding myself getting my third strike. This time it was for not being able to pick up the bits from the carpet in a timely manner. No, it was not a timely manner; it was an impossible task that he knew I would always fail.

"What am I going to do with you?" his chilling mechanical voice asked, staring aimlessly at me while he pondered what punishment would be suitable. "I think fifty slashes across the backside would do, don't you think, Sarah?"

Was he really asking Sarah this question? He continued to stare at me with his cold blank gaze, no doubt to see my reaction at him asking Sarah whether I should receive this punishment.

I continued to stay on all fours, the same position I'd been in for the past half an hour, and slowly glanced over to Sarah. She was doing as I thought, continuing to keep her head full force to her chin and staring coldly at the floor, tears beginning to stream one by one down her silky face and onto the carpet. This was bad, I thought – if Sarah was crying, I was sure to receive this punishment.

Then, in what seemed like slow motion, he spoke, relishing every word. "Well, that does it then. Stand up, the both of you – Kelly, you over here, and as you didn't answer, Sarah, you can watch."

I slowly got up, my legs turning to jelly as the panic set in, as well as the realisation that I was about to get fifty smacks. My every move towards him was torture, as every bone in my body wanted to run away and scream, but I'd contemplated doing this so many times before and had never actually done it.

The realisation always hit me: there was no one here to help me, and where would I run to anyway? So, I did the only thing I could – I let my solemn tears flow as I nervously continued to walk his way.

"Pants down and bend over," he ordered.

By now the tears were streaming full force down my face, and knowing what was about to happen, I started imagining the pain I was going to feel across my bare bottom – before he'd even started.

Mummy paced back and forth from the living room to the kitchen – looking troubled and pained, her stride uneasy – yet said nothing.

I watched Greg pull his belt from his trousers – it was a thick black belt with a large silver buckle attached to the end, the sight sending shudders down my spine.

I glanced at Sarah who stood opposite me, her face as white as death as she stared at me with sorrowful eyes. I then bent over the couch, using both hands to support my upper weight as he embraced the belt, wrapping a portion of it around his hand. The anticipation of waiting for him to start rippled right through me, enhancing my tears even further. I wailed loudly in the hope that Mummy would stop this, but still she did nothing.

He ordered me to count with each strike I was to receive.

"One!" I yelped as the striking began, the sharp slashes leaving a cold burning sensation on my skin. "Two!" I continued, as the sting increased with every strike. "Ow, three!" I screamed out, moving my hands to my bottom to try and protect it. I couldn't continue counting through the pain; each lash felt like it was tearing through my skin. With every strike my body jolted forward and the muscles in my bottom clenched, awaiting the next strike. The impulse to raise my hand to my bottom after every strike was stopped by Greg, prolonging the next strike he was to give. Numbness began to swell my mind, and I cried profusely as my bottom started to feel like it was on fire. I'd just started to slump slowly down to the floor from the couch, begging for the pain to stop, when he grabbed me by the scruff of the neck and slumped me back over the couch so he could continue.

I felt venomous and angry. I wanted to grab the belt and strike back at him, he who viciously tore huge chunks of my soul from me.

He continued to do the counting as he carried on whipping, though his voice became muffled and unclear – all I could hear was the sounds of my own crying.

Eventually the striking of the belt came to a halt and he told me to get up. My face was swollen and wet from the tears, and I wiped strands of hair away from around my eyes and cheeks.

I tried to clasp my bottom with my hands, but it felt too hot and only seemed to increase the burning pain. So instead I stood up in shock, feeling vulnerable as I attempted to pull my pants very carefully up my burning bottom – it was on fire, like it was full of hatred.

Then I heard Mummy's voice, sadly ordering Sarah and me to our room. I looked up to respond and saw her staring at my broken bottom, her face collapsed. Was she upset? I hadn't heard that tone in her voice since Germany.

I walked solemnly back to our bedroom, Sarah by my side. Every stride intensified the stinging on my bottom as it rubbed against my pants, a reminder of what had just happened. With every second that passed, my bottom was getting hotter and hotter.

Once I reached my room, the tears flowed more easily down my cheeks as I finally had the chance to mourn over the fifty lashes I'd just received. Slowly,

I released my pants from around my waist, allowing the heat to escape as the cool air hit my bottom. Sarah stood silent for a moment, her gaze dropping before me like a broken branch. My bottom and leg were lined with deep, enraged, red stained belt imprints. Scarcely an inch could be seen of faultless, imperforated skin as blood began to seep over my expanding wound.

I could see the concern in her eyes as she pulled in her breath to contain her whimpers. "It will be alright, Sarah," I murmured bravely, immediately stopping my tears to try and console her.

"It looks bad, Kelly – have you seen the side of your leg?" she protested.

The whipping from the belt had left lines of swollen skin and bruises all across my bottom and my thigh, but I hadn't noticed my thigh!

As I tried to sit on the edge of the bed I winced; I couldn't sit down. What was I going to do if I couldn't sit down? I had school the next day – what was I going to say to my teachers? Did I need to let them know I was bad and that's why I was unable to sit down? All these questions raced through my mind. At the age of eleven, I was more worried about what other people might think of me than being worried about myself.

"Why don't you lie on your side, Kelly?" Sarah

suggested. Clearly, I couldn't continue to stand all evening.

Slowly, I lay my head on the pillow. My mind was hollow. I had no hope, no joy, and no aspirations. I felt as though I was deflated. I had no voice, and no one cared. Sarah and I didn't know what we were going to do, though we discussed it until we were called for tea.

I got up out of bed to find a loose pair of pyjama bottoms to put on, and as I anxiously walked to the kitchen table where my dinner lay, Mummy approached me and asked to see my bottom.

Why? I thought to myself. She didn't care. She'd just watched as he whipped me fifty times across the backside. But I didn't dare let rip the questions that burnt inside of me, so I just responded with a, "Yes Mummy."

"Right, OK, pull your pants back up and sit down for tea," she said.

"I can't, Mummy," I responded in a shallow voice, so as not to be heard by him.

"What do you mean, you can't?" she snapped.

"It hurts when I sit down," I explained.

"OK, well stand and eat your dinner then," she said in a clammy and uncaring tone.

She left the kitchen to join Greg, and as I looked over at my dinner that I didn't want to eat, I could hear them talking. I couldn't afford another strike, so I stood to eat my dinner in silence.

Mummy was telling him that I had physical education this week and that I would have to wear shorts. She was concerned that the teachers would see my bruises. Her voice crackled; she had no confidence about her. She was advising him, rather than telling him.

Quietness fell upon the living room then, and I knew he was about to enter the kitchen.

Sure enough he appeared, pulling a chair out from beneath the table and slowly sitting down, then he proceeded to tell me that I wouldn't be going to school tomorrow.

I didn't know whether to feel happy or sad about this. I didn't want to have to tell school what had happened, but I also hated being at home.

His eyes stared long and dark at Sarah as she placed her fork down on the plate and removed her hands, placing them on her lap.

"Sarah, you will tell school that Kelly has the flu, and that this is the reason she will not be going in. Do you understand?"

I stared at Sarah, who raised her head up from her chest and replied, "Yes sir."

He then looked at me and said, "If you hadn't been naughty and got your three strikes then I wouldn't have had to punish you, do you understand?"

"Yes sir," I replied. What else was I to say? No, you mean monster? Every inch of my body despised him. I didn't even like looking at him; I felt nothing but hatred towards this man. It was clear that he hated us, and we hated him!

Finally, we were excused from the table. By now he knew he didn't have to say much to us, to convince us to do as we were told –he knew we feared him, and we knew what punishment we'd get if we defied him.

The next day, I was lonely.

I watched through the living room window as Sarah headed off to school. I felt venomous towards her just because she was able to go to school and get out of this rancid house. I watched until I couldn't see her anymore, her tiny self disappearing around the corner and away from the square, then I managed to grasp a little excitement from within. When she finished school, I would stand there and wait until I could spot her coming back.

Why, I thought to myself, was I now feeling this way towards Sarah? It wasn't her fault.

Luckily for me, Greg and Mummy were at work during the day and I was given permission to lie on the couch (on one side of my body) to watch television.

He left me alone for the next couple of days. There was no punishment and no strikes to abide by, probably because he knew I was in too much pain to carry out any tasks he wanted to set me. However, when he entered the room, I always knew my place. I would get up from where I lay and move to the chair, making sure that I was as quiet as a mouse. He didn't speak a word to me or Sarah over those days; if he wasn't punishing us or using us for his amusement then he didn't really have much to say to us. He would always say that we should be seen and not heard, though I often thought that was a lie – he didn't want to see us either.

CHAPTER NINE

THE RESCUE

THE DAYS SEEMED to drag, as did the healing of my bruises. My bottom and my thigh had a yellow tinge to them, so I knew it wouldn't be too long before most of the bruising would become unnoticeable.

School had just finished, so I watched through the window yet again as Sarah strode around the corner. I noticed she was walking faster than usual, and I waited for her, feeling anxious. She ran up the stairs, panic-stricken, her face riddled with worry.

"What's the matter, Sarah?" I shouted.

With trembling fingers she handed me a small card that was clasped in the palm of her hand. "I found this at the door," she said. It had been posted through the letterbox.

The card was from the National Society for the Prevention of Cruelty to Children, and a note was attached, advising that they'd visited today, but that no one was in.

"What! Where has this come from?" I said out loud. I was analysing the card, flipping it over back and forth, utterly confused.

Her face pale, Sarah stuttered some words that sent shivers running down my back. "I've told the teacher what happened, Kelly – they didn't believe me when I told them you'd had the flu for all this time." Her voice crumbled with instant regret of having said anything at all.

"What have you done, Sarah?" I snapped. "We're going to be in so much trouble – how do we explain this?"

Clearly distraught, her blue eyes went wild. "We could hide it where we hide our potato peel and not say anything," she suggested.

"No!" I slammed back. By now my chest was pounding, my heart racing at the very idea of punishment; he was sure to beat us black and blue for this. I fired questions at her, trying to make sense of all this. "Why did you tell the teacher? And what exactly did you tell her?"

"Everything!" Sarah cried. "It's not right what Greg's doing to us, Kelly, and I don't want to be here anymore!"

I was overridden by panic, the fear forcing me to lose all sense of direction. "OK, well we'll give it to him and see what happens – that's all we can do."

It felt like the longest time ever waiting for him and Mummy to return home, and the more I sat and waited, the more my body began to shake. When they did, I was sure my heart skipped a beat – several, in fact.

Sarah and I positioned ourselves on the chair with our hands on our knees, sitting still like mannequins displaying clothing for sale in a shop window, only I was unkempt-looking, and Sarah was in her school uniform.

To my surprise, I heard unfamiliar voices making their way up the stairs, voices that got louder and clearer the nearer they got to the living room.

"Hello girls," said one of the unfamiliar voices. There were two of them, and they were with Greg and Mummy. "This is Roger and I'm Tanya, and we are from the National Society for the Prevention of Cruelty to Children. We would like to have a chat with both of you if that's OK?"

I glanced briefly at Greg, who looked stern and unforgiving, and my lips quivered as I nodded my head in approval. Mummy stood like a statue with her head lowered down to her chin, her eyes coldly staring at the floor in shame.

Tanya was rather tall and had brown curly hair that resembled Sarah's. I studied this tall woman, taking in her posture and her clothing. She looked very well dressed, and everything about her appeared to be soft and yielding. She also had wonderful shoes, which I envied.

How beautiful, I thought – her high heels enhanced her height even further. They were the kind of heels I'd always dreamt of wearing, and they brought back memories of being at Nanny's house, strutting across the floor in my plastic teacup, pretending to be all grown up.

Roger was suited, slim, and also had dark hair. He wore polished shoes – though not as polished as Daddy's, no one could ever beat him at that. He was slightly smaller than Tanya, though that was probably because of her heels. I imagined her to be the one in charge, considering he would have to look up slightly in order to acknowledge and respond to her.

I stood there nervously, staring intently at them both. I couldn't make out the words in the conversation; I was too busy forbidding the tears to well in my eyes.

I could sense the awkwardness in the room. No

one was invited to sit down, and whenever small talk wasn't taking place, the room filled with deadly silence.

"Can we go to another room, please, to talk to the girls?" Tanya asked, looking at Greg to be shown where we could go.

"Why do you need another room? Why can't you talk to them here?" he asked, as cowardly as a rat.

"It's procedure," Roger answered. "We would like to talk to them privately, just to ask them a few questions."

With a slight hesitation, Greg announced that the kitchen would be a good place to chat.

Was he scared, I wondered? Or was he seething with that much anger that we were sure to get it when they left? I didn't want to think about that last one too much.

We followed Roger and Tanya to the kitchen, where I stood stiffly, blinking back my tears as the door shut quickly behind me.

Tanya knelt on her knees and took both my hands into the palm of her hands; they were as soft as spring. She seemed as if she was caring, and she managed to move me with her tantalising eyes. She leaned towards me, pulling back one hand to tenderly push the curls away from her face.

Firstly, she explained why she was here, and then she asked us to explain what was going on in the home.

I couldn't speak. I was mute, my voice screaming inside my head that he was in the next room – I was conscious that he could hear everything. I imagined his stone-cold eyes glinting with disapproval, a fixed scowl etched on his face. He was surely sitting there right now planning our punishment, preparing his weapons to beat us with. Who was going to save us when they left?

Yet Sarah seemed to have none of these problems, none of these worries. She simply roared, like an active volcano that continued to spit out the cruel works of Greg.

She told them the truth – the whole truth. Naked, cold, and fatal like a blade she continued, unable to spit her words out fast enough.

I watched in amazement at the bravery she displayed, in trying to save the both of us.

"Can I have a look at your leg?" Tanya whispered to me in her soft tone, so tantalising – I hadn't heard that tone in a long time. A nice, warm, caring tone.

I nodded yes, thinking that I had to stick by Sarah now and show them proof of what was happening. So, standing firmly like a rooted tree, I pulled my bottoms part way down my leg to show Tanya, though I wasn't exactly hopeful. I didn't know what to expect or what was going to happen, but I did know that Greg was sitting there in the living room with Mummy, ready to pronounce a whole year's worth of strikes.

"What about George?" Roger asked. "Does anything ever happen to him?"

"No, never," Sarah responded. Her eyes were wide, full of hope and with a glint of excitement, yet she stood helpless and vulnerable.

Once Sarah had finished telling them our story, we were asked politely to stay in the kitchen while they went and spoke to Mummy and Greg.

My eyes flashed to Sarah, to ask her what she thought was going to happen.

"I told the truth, Kelly, that's all that matters," she told me.

I was just so amazed at her strength and courage. Why didn't I have this courage? She knew that what was happening to us was wrong, and yet I thought this went on in all homes.

As I stood alone with Sarah in the kitchen, waiting for the door to reopen, it seemed like an eternity was passing. What was taking them so long?

We continued to stand in silence, praying they wouldn't leave us alone another night with that monster. It was clear Mummy couldn't protect us, so they had to do it instead, right?

The more I thought about him entering the room, the more my leg began to twitch until it was almost uncontrollable. My thoughts started to expand unmanageably as I imagined what punishment we would receive. I prayed silently that this would all just disappear. By now I was in more anguish than ever and my jerky movements began to get the better of me.

The door opened and there stood Tanya to greet us, while Roger stood in the background next to Greg.

"We're going now, Kelly and Sarah," she said to us, "but we'll see you again soon, OK?"

I frowned, the bones in my body feeling as though they were about to crumple, my forbidden tears ripping loose. I felt sick to my stomach. They were leaving us! Leaving us to deal with Greg's wrath once they'd left.

Sarah's face was white as a ghost as she also realised we were going to be left behind. She looked to me for comfort, for me to save her, but there was nothing I could do.

We said our shallow goodbyes to them, not knowing whether we would ever see them again, and remained frozen in the same spot while Mummy and Greg escorted them downstairs to let them out. We were alone.

Then, when they reappeared (and without notice), Greg seized Sarah around the neck and threw her from where she stood, right over to the couch. Within seconds he used his same hand to throw a hard slap across my face. The sting didn't seem so bad as I watched him storm over to Sarah, before she even had a chance to get up from the couch. His face was seething in anger. A tempest of hot rage had taken hold of him, changing his face from a constant blank stare with hollow eyes, to a face of fire.

He pounced on her like a cat pouncing on its prey. My tears were summoned by him once again, feeling hopeless while he pulled on her hair and knocked his head against hers, so that his nose stayed firmly fixed on hers while he screamed, "What have you done?"

Mummy blazed in then, with unexpected flare, "That's enough now, Greg, it's done."

He climbed from Sarah. By now his face was bulging like a man possessed, his glasses crooked from his nose, having forgotten to remove these before he pounced. "Get out of my sight, both of you!"

I began to run as I saw Sarah remove herself from the couch. I ran as if my life depended on it, all the way to my bedroom, with Sarah in tow. Once we reached our bedroom, we closed the door in the hope that we wouldn't be disturbed for the rest of the night. We didn't move, breathe heavily, or whisper; we simply sat very quietly on the edge of the bed whilst we tried to comprehend what had just happened.

Sarah eventually broke the silence – with all the commotion, she realised that we hadn't had anything to eat, but I didn't mind. We always had a supply of potato peels in our room and knew that we could eat those if we wanted to, but I was too scared to move from the bed in case he wasn't quite finished with us.

So, we continued to just sit there on the edge of the bed, silent and terrified.

It seemed like an endless day, but soon I noticed that it was getting dark. Growing sleepier and sleepier, I finally whispered that it was time to get ready for bed.

Sarah nodded her head in agreement and started to take her uniform off, which she was still wearing from when she'd returned from school earlier.

We then crawled into bed, trying to get warm; the night seemed like a dreary, cold night. Nestling down together, we said our goodnights and talked of dreaming sweet dreams, where our problems would not live.

The next morning Mummy came into our room and asked us to get ready, including me. It was time for me to return to school.

This was it, I thought to myself – everything is going to go back to normal, and he might even leave us alone for a bit in fear that the same man and woman might turn up again. I could only hope.

The morning walk to school felt like any other morning, and we both giggled at the sight of Greg when he'd been asked if we could go into the kitchen.

"His face was riddled with fear!" I giggled.

He was a bully, but for a split second I almost felt sorry for him as his face dropped like a sack of potatoes when he'd been confronted by Roger and Tanya.

School felt different. I was greeted by the teacher in a way she'd never greeted me before. She talked to me with such pleasantries, care, and compassion that she almost seemed alien to me.

As lunchtime approached two familiar faces appeared in the hall. It was Roger and Tanya, paying a visit to check that me and Sarah were OK. Tanya placed herself next to me at the dinner table and began to ask how everything had gone the night before at home when they'd left.

I continued to eat my jam sandwiches that Mummy had prepared for me, as I pondered how I was going to answer this question.

Sarah, who had Roger sitting beside her, seemed to be chatting away like she was relaying a fun-filled day to him. I wanted to scream at her, 'Stop! Look at the trouble we got into last night! If he finds out they've been here to the school, the pain we'd suffer would be unimaginable!'

Disregarding my sulkiness, Tanya repeated the question to me, but all I could think of was to say it was fine. Her presence made me feel uneasy. I sat trying to eat my lunch as quickly as possible, so that I could leave the table sooner. I didn't know why they were here, especially as they'd left us with him last night after everything Sarah had told them, so why would it be any different today? The hope and trust that someone was going to rescue us from him had diminished instantly the second they walked out of that door. My trust was broken, like broken bones that would heal but would never be the same again. All I could think of was that it would be home time soon and that we were the ones who had to face him, not them.

Flutters of panic set in slowly as it got nearer to home time. I hadn't seen Greg since the night before, and I wondered how he was going to react when we got home. The anxiety crept in slowly, like a snake slithering up my body from beneath me, working its way to my chest where it would slowly wrap itself around me, each squeeze tormenting me with suffocation. Fear. That's what it was. I lived and breathed constant fear of him.

When the last bell rang for home time, I waited for Sarah as I did every day. I didn't know whether Roger and Tanya were still there, and I didn't care; I just wanted to get home and be done with whatever punishment I had coming. Me and Sarah exchanged a smile, a silent promise that we were going to survive this together and get through the night, as we approached our front door.

Opening the door and walking up the stairs towards the living room, I could hear voices in the distance. Mummy was sitting on the single chair, stiff-jointed and upset, with her frail, bloated face in her hands. Mummy must not have gone to work today; she was never normally home when we got back from school.

Staring at Mummy, I wondered what the matter was. I considered going over to tentatively hug her, but I couldn't bring myself to do so. My snide thoughts ran about me, preventing me from approaching her.

Mummy continued to sit in the chair that me and Sarah would usually sit in, while I just stood next to Sarah, feeling lost. We normally composed ourselves in that very chair Mummy was sitting in now, in readiness for whenever Greg arrived home.

He then emerged from the kitchen with a grave look of disappointment and disgust on his face as he stared over at us. His mouth opened gormlessly and, full of hatred, he said, "Look at how upset your mother is – you've both done this to her and I don't want to look at either of you right now."

Mummy peered up at him, her eyes swollen, looking defeated and humbled. She didn't look at us, clearly didn't want to meet our eyes, and to think I'd contemplated hugging her!

He walked slowly towards us, then instructed us

both to follow. I wished nothing more but to be out of his sight, but my wishes never amounted to much. Then he opened the dreaded cupboard to the boiler. I didn't need to look at Sarah; I could already hear her sniffles begin when she realised he was sending us to the one place she feared the most.

Squeezing into one side of the cupboard, I wondered whether I would fit now – I seemed to have grown since the last time I'd entered this cupboard. I cuddled my legs up towards my chest to allow room for Sarah to crawl in, and sitting opposite her, I tried to calm her by telling her to ignore the sounds of the boiler that stood between us. She was crying, fat tears streaming down her flawless face. My snide thoughts were still about me, and I couldn't help but feel resentment towards her. After all, what did she think was going to happen? We were never going to be rescued, and I could think of a lot worse things he could have done this evening as punishment.

I sat pondering why Mummy had been crying. Was she crying out of pity for me and Sarah? If she was, she'd never done it before, had never seemed to care enough to do it before.

Once Sarah had exhausted her tears and began to settle, I asked her what she'd told Roger in the dinner hall at school.

She spoke mercilessly. "I told him the truth, Kelly,

about what Greg did to me when they left. He told me they'd be at school every day to talk to us, to make sure we're OK."

"To make sure we're OK, Sarah?" I responded in a callous tone. "Sarah, we're *not* OK, but it doesn't matter – they're not doing anything, so what's the point in talking to them?"

"Please, Kelly, just tell them the truth. If you do, we might have a chance to get Greg out of this house and away from us."

She was pleading with me to cooperate and help her. She just looked so pained, and her cry sent shivers down my spine.

"OK Sarah," I said after a moment, "I'll do what you're asking, but I just don't know what they can do. I mean, they left us here with him last night and look what he did!"

A glimmer of hope sparkled over Sarah's eyes, leaving me to feel proud for just a moment at being able to soothe her, keeping her attention drawn away from what stood between us. Now all we had to do was sit and wait to be let out.

A couple of hours later, the door began to open unusually slowly, and Mummy appeared from behind the door, frail and drawn-looking. "Get yourself to bed, girls," she said in a shallow, timid voice.

I hesitated to move, not knowing whether to take

requests from Mummy as gospel. She didn't tell us what to do; he did.

"Well, come on then," she commanded, waving her hand towards us to hurry up. "Greg has fallen asleep and it's getting late."

I was stiff and my bottom numb from sitting in such a cramped space, so I did as I was told.

Mummy left as soon as me and Sarah entered our bedroom, but I didn't care – I was used to putting myself to bed and not having anyone to say good-night to other than Sarah.

As I lay my head on the pillow, I thought about keeping my promise to Sarah. I really didn't want to engage in any more conversations with Tanya and Roger, but I would for my sister, to show her that we weren't going to get anywhere with this.

The next morning at school I actively went to seek out Tanya at lunchtime. Right, I thought to myself, I'll tell her what's been going on. She sat next to me, just as she had the day before, and I began to tell her about the three strikes that me and Sarah lived by every day.

I couldn't believe that I was talking, and once I'd started, I found I couldn't get my words out quick enough. They were rolling off my tongue as I relayed all the bad things he liked to do to us, with an angry broken roar to my tone as I expressed my pure hatred for this man. My uttering words sounded like wild cries, like a creature in pain. I didn't care who heard me and I didn't stop to even take a breath, for fear that she would interrupt me. With strength like steel, I spat out as much information about this man as I could, to ensure that she had a clear picture of what he was truly like. I was impressed, awed, and yet terrified of what would happen next, having realised everything I'd just told her.

She placed her soft hand on mine and began to talk. Her words were always like honey that melted from a comb, so caring and so concerned about letting me know she'd taken in every word I'd just expressed.

Yet I couldn't help but feel as though I had a frog stuck in my throat, realising that everything I'd just said would surely get back to him. He knew everything. He had eyes and ears in the back of his head. Had I just set myself up for further strikes and punishment? Had I just been duped into telling her everything?

The rest of the afternoon went far too fast, imagining him waiting for me at home and all the cruel things he was going to do to me, once he found out what I'd just done.

I wasn't at all eager to get home, so I strolled back from school at a slow pace, for my legs wouldn't let me go any faster. Panic set in like a thump to the chest, as I was convinced he knew. My imagination began to run wild, picturing him standing there with his buckled belt wrapped around both hands, pulling his hands in and out across his chest so that I would hear sounds of the leather snapping back as the belt straightened. What have I done? I couldn't face another whipping.

"What's the matter, Kelly? You haven't spoken a word to me all the way home," Sarah muttered in complaint.

"I'm fine," I mumbled back, "I'm just wondering whether Greg's at home." I was petrified at the thought of him being in the flat, yet I couldn't tell her this. I worried enough for the both of us.

He was home! My legs felt like lead as I climbed the stairs to the living room. His presence made my skin crawl, leaving the whole of my body trembling as I approached him. I was sure he would know just by looking at me; I could not stop my jittering body from shaking.

"I'm in the mood for a fight," he said as he removed his glasses from his face and placed them down onto the table.

I watched in terror while he moved the furniture to make room for what was about to happen. I stared at him, intensifying my hatred with every glance he made towards me.

Maybe my eyes were like ice, chilling and cold revealing the years I sort for revenge. He was a giant worm that crawled out from beneath the soil, cowardly, leaving behind his castings – with no purpose – upon his prey.

Rage started to fill me, and my earlier conversation with Tanya couldn't be further from my mind. I would not give him the satisfaction of seeing me cry, not again, not like the feeble weakling he liked to think I was.

So, I placed my school bag down and took off my coat, hoping he wouldn't notice that I'd left my shoes on. He wanted a fight; I would do my best to give him one. I had to make sure he didn't get me to the ground, however, knowing that I couldn't bear the thought of his grubby hands over my mouth and nose. If Sarah could do it, then so could I.

Crouching down to the floor, his bone-chilling eyes stared at me. He didn't need to talk to give me permission to strike at him; his eyes said it all.

I approached, my anger raging and roaring inside me, making my blood boil. I clenched my fists as I stood determinedly before him, daring and challenging him to do his worst. He covered his face with both fists in readiness for my strike. Then, like an enraged tiger, I struck with one hand towards his face. I also kicked him in the chest, hard, and with as much force as I could muster, pushing him back from his crouching position and onto his back. Today I would deny this detestable man my blood. Today, I would fight back.

I continued to punch his vulnerable face that he'd left wide open for my attack, all the anger rushing out of me like a tornado from a storm. I had learnt by now that I received beatings regardless of whether I fought back or not, so my only chance was to fight. The force behind my punches kept him down on the floor, and I continued to kick and hit with all my might, making sure it wasn't me on my back, when eventually he said, "Enough!"

Never again would I feel pity for him, pity for Mummy, or pity for myself. I was done.

I moved back far enough so that he couldn't reach me, pulling my matted hair away from my neck as I did so. My cheeks were hot to the touch, most probably stained red, and burning the tips of my fingers.

He got up. The eagerness had faded from his eyes, leaving them as cold as the winter sky after a snowy day. He continued to stare at me as he pulled himself together, a surprising gaze in his eyes. Clearly, he had wanted to make me come undone this night, but his attempts had failed.

I was surprised at myself, and so was he – he hadn't expected the courage I displayed for myself and

Sarah. He wanted to wither my soul, making me feel small and dull, but not today, as I felt pretty good. Not today, would he steal the power of life from me. Not today, was he going to steal the power of death from me. Not today, not while I could fight back.

My mood started to even out when Mummy arrived home from work. I wasn't sure I could perform like that again, as my anger washed away like the high tide recoiling back to the sea.

"What's been going on?" Mummy asked, as if it wasn't obvious from the misplaced furniture.

"I've been fighting with Kelly and she did very well," Greg explained, like I had just earnt a small amount of respect from him.

For once, we could eat dinner with no interference of any punishment. I continued to keep my guard up, though, even as I sat and ate my dinner. You could never tell what he might decide to do next.

The following day was like any other; we attended school and sat at lunchtime to talk to Roger and Tanya. I was still unsure of why they were there, as everything was OK at school. I didn't fear school or anyone in it, only home – and there was always a big bad man waiting for us at home.

I had forgotten about everything I'd told Tanya, and headed home once school had finished. We were to have breaded drumsticks for tea that evening;

Mummy asked Sarah to go and grab them out of the chest freezer whilst she finished taking the rest of George's uniform off.

Still reeling in my victory from the night before, I worked my way into the kitchen to assist Sarah, when suddenly she dropped the opened bag of chicken drumsticks on the floor.

"Get those picked up!" Greg shouted at her.

As Sarah bent down to pick the chicken up from the floor, Greg placed his heavy toe-capped work boots over her hand, which was placed on the floor. He then twisted and grinded his foot, like he wanted to bury her hand beneath the floorboards, making her scream out, "Ow!"

His face mimicked his foot, twisted and coiled with pursed lips, with every intent to show her who had authority. Then, as quickly as he'd stamped on her hand, he callously lifted his foot again.

Tears were streaming down Sarah's face as she wailed pitifully, but although she was in pain, she continued to pick up the chicken with her other hand.

Mummy came running into the kitchen and asked what the matter was, and Greg – his voice cold, yet somehow convincing to Mummy – went on to explain that he'd accidently stood on Sarah's hand.

Well, I knew this wasn't true, as I'd witnessed his demonic handiwork, just like all the other times. I waited in the hope she would ask me what had happened, but she didn't. She just turned on her heel and spun back around to the living room to attend to George.

Soon it was dinner time, and Sarah continued to sob. Unable to use the fingers on her one hand, she placed her hand in her lap and used her unharmed hand to eat her food. Greg was out – he had decided to go for a few drinks with his so-called friends. I could see that Sarah didn't want to eat her dinner, and who could blame her after what she'd just endured?

After dinner I helped Mummy clear the plates away, while Sarah sat in the living room, clutching her hand – a sight I'd been familiar with a few years back when Greg had burnt her hand.

Mummy eventually got around to asking why she was still crying.

"My fingers hurt, Mummy," Sarah replied, "it feels like I've got pins stabbing my fingers." She sniffed, pointing to the last two fingers on her left hand.

Mummy's weary, unbelieving eyes stared at Sarah's fingers long enough to inspect them. Sarah lifted her gaze to stare into Mummy's eyes, wanting to be reassured, but she wasn't.

"It was an accident, Sarah; I'm sure they'll be fine in the morning," she snapped at her, before turning her back on her in the hope the complaint would vanish.

"No, Mummy!" I shouted back. "He purposely stood on her fingers when she dropped the chicken on the floor."

She huffed, clearly not wanting to hear it. She never wanted to hear anything we had to say, especially if it involved him.

My eyes widened in shock at the realisation that Mummy was mean too – perhaps just as mean as him.

"Both of you go to bed please," she sneered in a callous and disbelieving way. She was a beaten-down woman, all hope lost. It wasn't like she'd done everything in her power to make things right and to fight for us – she'd done nothing. The truth was she simply didn't care. Why did she look so torn and drained, then, the tiredness putting years on her face?

We did as we were told and headed towards our bedroom, where I tried to calm Sarah down, telling her it would hopefully feel better in the morning. I couldn't console her any more than that, as the truth was, I didn't know what else to say. The least I could do was help her get undressed; her fingers had seemed to swell, and I could see the strain on her face through the struggle of trying to take her jumper off. How could Mummy not care about that? You could plainly see the pain she must be in.

During the night I was woken by her sniffles.

"It hurts, Kelly. I'm sorry that I woke you," she said in the most apologising way.

"It's OK, it will soon be school time and I'm sure the teacher will look at it for you."

"OK," she replied quietly.

"Now try and get some sleep if you can," I added, trying my very best to let her know it would be OK. But I wasn't sure myself whether *anything* would be OK. Again, Mummy had proved that she didn't care and so there was no one to turn to but each other. If I could have taken the pain away from my sister, I would have done.

The next morning, we got up and I helped Sarah to get dressed. The pain had subsided a little, she explained, but she couldn't bend her fingers.

"Don't say anything to Mummy, Sarah, or Greg might not let you go to school, like I wasn't allowed to go to school. And you need some cream on your fingers, which you can get from school," I encouraged her.

Sitting in class, I wondered how she was getting on – I'd left her in the hallway to make her own way to her class. I wondered whether by now she'd had the cream she needed to get her fingers right again. I continued to stare at the teacher aimlessly, and a few moments later Tanya knocked and entered the classroom.

"Hello Miss, would it be OK if I took Kelly out of class to have a word?" she asked.

"Yes, of course – go ahead Kelly," she replied, using her hands to wave at me, directing me out of class.

I was confused. As I stood from my chair and proceeded to the classroom door, I wondered if I'd done something wrong.

I nervously followed Tanya to the entrance where the headmaster's office lay, wracking my brains, going over the last few days' events to work out what I'd said or done to be taken out of class. My life was full of bad surprises that always involved me getting into trouble, so why would now be any different?

Approaching the office, I saw Sarah and Roger sitting there, waiting for us. Tanya explained that we weren't in any trouble, but that we needed to go to the hospital to get Sarah's fingers looked at by a doctor.

"Oh, OK, yes," I responded in a surprised voice. I'd been convinced I was in trouble.

As I nervously sat in the hospital waiting room with Tanya (while Roger took Sarah in to be seen by the doctor), it suddenly dawned on me that we'd get in a lot of trouble for being here. "How long are we going to be, Tanya?" I asked nervously. "Because Mummy and Greg don't know where we are and if we're not home when we're supposed to be, we'll be in a lot of trouble."

"It's OK, Kelly," she stated calmly, "we've told Mummy and Greg where you are, so don't worry about that please."

No! I thought to myself, knowing we'd be in even more trouble now; I hadn't realised that they knew already.

I began to feel my legs twitching while I impatiently waited for Sarah to return. How long was she going to be? She only needed some cream, surely? At least if we got back before school finished, Greg might be lighter on us with the punishment – perhaps.

The panic set in then, my breathing increasing whilst my chest tightened, my legs uncontrollably twitching and moving, clearly wanting to run from this place and go straight back home.

"Kelly, it's going to be OK, trust me," said Tanya, placing her hand on my knee in an attempt to calm me down.

Roger appeared on his own from the room where he'd taken Sarah, yet there was no Sarah. He greeted Tanya and me and said, "Sarah has dislocated fingers, so they're just strapping them up. Are you OK to wait here with the girls?"

I stood from my chair. "Where are you going?" I yelped.

"I'm going to sort some things out, and go and speak to Mummy and Greg," he said in the gentlest way possible.

"No!" I raged. "Last time you left us there and went home he was really mean to us, and when we go home tonight he's going to be very angry with us for being here, for talking to you!" I was frantic, crying and pleading with them just to take us home, sorry that I'd told Sarah to get some cream off the teacher. I felt as though the whole world was crashing down around my shoulders, pulling me down to the ground – and no one was listening!

Tanya pulled me into her arms and to her chest. Burying my head there, I cried furiously. "It will be OK this time, I promise," she said in a soothing voice. "Let Roger go off to sort things, while we sit and wait for Sarah."

"OK," I sniffled, realising I had no choice; I would just have to sit and wait it out, and train my mind for the worst possible punishment I might receive once I got home.

Sarah was eventually escorted back to us by the doctor, her fingers wrapped in white cloth.

"Does it still hurt?" I asked, while Tanya stood to one side, talking to the doctor.

"No, it's much better now. Where's Roger?" she asked.

"I don't know, but we have to get home soon;

it's getting dark outside and we have school tomorrow," I said, sounding more concerned about school than home.

After what seemed like hours – during which my thoughts took frantic flight, wanting to escape this hospital and return home –Roger eventually returned to us at the hospital with a smug, satisfied smile on his face.

He seemed happy as he approached me and Sarah, then he crouched down in front of us to give us some news. "I have been away to find you a new home. You can go there tonight – they're a lovely couple called Sylvia and Gordon."

I felt overwhelmed, that for at least tonight I wouldn't have to endure the wrath of Greg, but what about tomorrow? "What about Mummy and Greg, and when we have to go home tomorrow?" I asked with dissatisfaction, thinking we were only saved for one night.

"No, Kelly, Mummy and Greg have been told that you won't be going home; you will stay with your new family for a little while, whilst we sort everything else out," Tanya explained.

CHAPTER TEN

FOSTER HOME

IN THAT MOMENT I felt weak with relief – finally, I could breathe again. I wondered, however, why they hadn't told us this before, making me panic for several hours for no reason.

"I couldn't say anything, not until I was sure I had a family for you to go home to tonight," Roger explained.

I was overjoyed, and clearly, so was my sister. I hadn't seen a smile on Sarah's face in such a long time; it was like a ray of sunshine beaming down from the heavens above.

"What about our clothes and our things?" I continued with my questions, sure there would be at least one hurdle I would have to overcome.

"Kelly, stop worrying. Your new family has clothes for you," Roger said, laughing, clearly proud of his achievement.

I felt a huge surge of happiness then, as if all my Christmases had come at once, despite having no memories of any previous Christmases. I hadn't experienced this feeling in a very long time.

Soon enough we were climbing into the back of Roger's car and heading for our new home. It hardly seemed real. What would these people be like? I wondered.

It was late and dark outside, and as I looked out the car window I asked, "Are you sure they're expecting us?" I still couldn't help but feel hesitation on the drive to our new home, concerned that my happiness was going to be short-lived. I found myself analysing all the possibilities of having to go back to Greg, especially as I'd spent most of the day mentally preparing myself for the next set of punishments.

"Yes, they're waiting for you as we speak," Tanya responded, in the hope that this would calm me down.

Approaching the house, I stared at all the big houses that were lined up in a row down the street. It was incredibly different to where Mummy and Greg lived.

Roger had just stopped and parked his car on the road in front of the house when the door suddenly flung open.

There stood a woman with short brown hair, who appeared to be very well dressed. She didn't stand at the door for any longer than was necessary, quickly walking over to us, both arms opened in a warm welcome.

As I continued to look over at the house, I saw a man standing hesitantly in the doorway. Some dogs from inside the home stood by his side, curious to see what all the commotion was about, wagging their tails in excitement.

Roger opened the car door to let us out and introduced us to Sylvia, who was really eager to meet us.

"Hello! Which one is Kelly?" she asked in a familiar accent I'd heard once before, many years ago in Germany.

I raised my hand in acknowledgement that this was me – I was still too scared to speak, wondering whether I was actually back at home and this was all just a dream.

"And so you must be Sarah," she said, bending down to be on her level so as not to intimidate her. "It's so nice to meet you both! Please, come with me and meet Gordon and my dogs."

I followed behind Sarah; she was so hopeful and trusting as she clung to Sylvia, who escorted her in.

"This is Gordon," she explained. A tall, stockier man with an articulate tone greeted us, also with open arms. "And let's not forget Lucy, Sally, and Tara," she continued as the dogs greeted us too, one of them even licking my hand. Tara was a black dog with a few straggly grey hairs. She must be old, I thought. Then there was Lucy and Sally, a small Yorkshire Terrier that yapped away at us, letting us know she was there. Well, I thought, I'd also yap loudly if I was that small.

Tenderly, Tanya took my hand to walk me through the front door.

I was greeted by stairs directly in front of me, which I assumed led to the bedrooms. To my left was a dining area with a huge dark oak table sitting directly in the middle of the room. Decorative candles were carefully placed on its surface. The room looked as though it was hardly ever touched, perhaps only being used on special occasions. Walking towards the stairs, to my left I was greeted by the kitchen. I had never seen such a large kitchen before, and I was mesmerised by all the crockery that sat perfectly in their places. We were then escorted to the right, where the living room lay. The room looked so modern. I was intrigued, not being able to spot anything that even resembled Mummy's house. There was no musty brown, not a single item. Instead, the room was filled with colour, and even flowers had been arranged accordingly in an expensive vase.

I could not believe the direction my eyes had

taken me: to another long table, this one full of goodies. Yes, just off the living room was a conservatory, where lots of amazing goodies greeted us. This room was full of books and games and must be used for fun and laughter, I thought to myself. Sylvia explained that she had made us chocolate sandwiches and that there were all sorts of cakes and biscuits for us to choose from – she hadn't been sure what we did and didn't like, so had got lots of different things just in case. I had never seen so many delights in my life. I could pick any one of these to eat, and as for the chocolate sandwiches, I had never tasted one before.

"Tuck in, girls, it's all for you," Sylvia said, her careful hands grabbing a plate to hand to me.

I watched Sarah. She didn't give it even a moment's thought before tucking in, while the adults went back into the living room to talk further. They were very quiet as they spoke, so as not to be overheard by Sarah and myself.

I took a moment to stare at Sarah, her face full of satisfaction while she stuffed a cake into her mouth. I could almost taste the cake she ate, for her smile gleamed so brightly.

I wondered for the moment whether this was all a trick. I felt spoilt. Did I really deserve all these delights that were staring at me, tantalising me and teasing me to eat them?

"Come on, Kelly, I can't eat all this by myself! Here, try the sandwich," Sarah said, rapidly handing me the sandwich as if it might disappear at any second.

I took the sandwich from her hand and took a bite. She was right – it tasted so good. I turned to look in the direction of the living room, catching Sylvia staring at us with a smile so pleasing to my eyes that I knew it was OK to continue eating, so I pulled out a chair to sit at the table.

Not too long after, Roger and Tanya had to say their goodbyes. They told us that they'd visit us in a couple of days to see how we were getting on, so I knew we had some time to relax and recharge before we had to go back to Mummy.

There was no awkwardness with Sylvia or Gordon, who made us feel very welcome as they showed us to our bedroom. Climbing up the stairs, we saw a huge bathroom full of light and a big open space on the right as we passed. Directly in front was Sylvia and Gordon's bedroom, then the guest room beside their room, and our room down the hall. We had bunkbeds and mine was the top bunk, as I was the older one. Directly in front of the bed were some empty drawers.

"They'll be filled with new clothes in no time, just you wait and see," Sylvia told us, her tone full of assurance. "Tomorrow we'll go out and get a few bits and bobs; you'll be pleased to know there'll be no school for a couple of days until things settle down."

I was delighted. If every day was going to be like this I didn't need to pine after school anymore! My terrible past would lie far, far away, like a dream left in the night.

The night had soon fallen upon us and Sylvia tucked us both up in bed. This felt alien to me; it had been a long time since Mummy had entered our room to help us to bed, let alone tuck our bed covers over and say goodnight.

Soon I was ready to fall asleep, with the comfort of my pillow in my fingers and my thumb in my mouth.

"Do you think Mummy's alright?" Sarah asked. She sounded content, but it was clear she needed reassuring with an answer in order for her to sleep.

"Yes, Sarah," I told her. "We have to think about ourselves now; we can no longer worry about him and Mummy."

"But what about George? I'm going to miss George."

My response felt callous as I went on to tell her that he would also be fine and that nothing ever happened to him as he was Greg's son.

I did my best as the older sister to put her mind at ease so that she could go to sleep. The truth was, I hadn't given them even one moment of thought after

Roger and Tanya left and I couldn't understand why she would.

The following morning, I was woken by Sylvia shouting for us – in a pleasant way – to come and join her for breakfast. Excitement ripped through Sarah as she tore off her covers and jumped out of bed. The glow in her eyes was different; I hadn't seen that in a long time and had forgotten what it looked like.

I cautiously followed Sarah down the stairs, not knowing what to expect. My chest didn't feel so tight that I couldn't breathe, but my stomach fluttered.

There, much to my surprise, spread out on the dark oval table was some tea and some funny-shaped bread, along with a pot of chocolate spread. I looked at the bread, playing with it in my hands, feeling the warmth, when Sylvia explained it was a croissant.

"Oh," I replied.

"Come on, eat up – we need to put some meat on those bones!" She giggled a bit like a school child, though I wondered if what she said was true – after all, for a long time we'd just been living off potato peels, whenever we were sent to bed without tea.

I certainly felt like royalty. It had been a very long time since I'd felt spoilt, though it still seemed very surreal and I wondered how long it would last.

After breakfast, Sylvia announced that we were

going shopping and that we'd take a walk together to get a few bits and bobs.

Getting dressed, I watched Sarah. She couldn't wait to get her trousers on due to the excitement that had taken hold of her. It was nice to see her happy for once.

'Come on, girls, are you ready?" Sylvia encouraged.

Running down the stairs, I realised this felt alien to me too – Mummy hadn't taken us out anywhere since Germany.

It felt surreal again as we stood on each side of Sylvia, holding her hand as we walked down the busy high street that had so many varieties of different shops. There were so many people shopping and looking happy – another thing I hadn't seen before.

As we entered the children's clothes shop Sylvia was excited, picking out tops and skirts for us to wear. Again, I felt like royalty. I stared at Sylvia as she intently picked out clothes, a glow in her eyes that lit up her face, placing them against our tiny bodies whilst she checked the sizing. It didn't take her long to select a few items of clothing for us both, and it seemed like she'd done this many times before.

A few days had passed, and Roger and Tanya came to pay us a visit. They carefully explained that they wanted us to go with them to the police station to make a statement and to tell the policeman everything that happened to us, as they believed Greg needed to be punished. With my thoughts turning to revenge, I felt more than happy to do this. I secretly imagined him doing push-ups and having to stand against the wall for hours – finally he would get to know what it felt like.

Everyone was very welcoming at the police station. The place was big yet plain and seemed to have a deep, lingering sense of coldness, like the cold breath of the grave. I was escorted into one room while Sarah was escorted into another.

Sitting down at the table, the nice policeman began writing. "Now, in your own words, can you explain what Greg has done to you?"

This was my moment. It took me back to when I'd spotted Sarah talking to Roger, like she was talking for England. I was only too happy to reel off everything Greg had done to us, my brain screaming for revenge. I wanted to see him locked up in prison, put behind bars and convicted of abusing two small girls. He would be the mouse that crept about in the dark, Only he would have a large gathering of men, men like him, most probably and undoubtable bullies, just as he was. He would have no trips to the pub with his friends, no privacy when he had his shower once a week. I was only too pleased with my unkind thoughts of him suffering, and for sure I would not visit him.

"Slow down," the policeman ordered with a slight chuckle to his speech; he couldn't keep up with his writing.

Soon my time had come to an end, which sparked a slight disappointment in me as I had so much more to say about this horrid man. For the first time, however, I felt relief, as the burden of keeping in what he'd done to us for so many years was finally gone. I had planned to tell Daddy, Caroline, Nanny, and Grandad on so many occasions but couldn't, yet I hadn't planned to tell the policeman and I did.

It was soon time to return to school. Sylvia reassured us both that she would be dropping and picking us up from school and that we had nothing to worry about. But I couldn't help but worry as I knew my home wasn't far from the school, which meant he wasn't far from me either.

As we approached the school, I couldn't help but feel anxious. I wondered where he was and what everyone at school thought about us, yet as the days went on, I became relaxed within my surroundings and found that home started to become nothing more than a distant memory.

I missed George. He was in the school next to mine and I would often bump into him in the playground and even in class, when he decided he was going to sneak out of his school and run across the field to reach me and Sarah. He would get a few seconds or even minutes with me sometimes, until his teacher came running into class to take him back to school for the umpteenth time.

Who could blame him? After all, he didn't have the faintest idea why me and Sarah had been ripped away from home, and he just wanted to be near us. All my resentment faded with George over time, and there was no doubt in my mind that he would be OK – I told myself that he was Greg's son and no harm had ever come to him, so that shouldn't change now.

I was just happy that me and Sarah were safe and didn't have to see Greg anymore – that was, until one day as I skipped about the playground when a familiar face approached the school gates, striding along the path.

I knew that stride and that build, and what had once faded in me returned in a flash. I found myself frozen where I stood, my feet not budging, like the sword in the stone waiting to be pulled out. It had been a while since my body felt this way, and I had almost forgotten the stresses my body had endured at his hands – until this very moment. Did he know that I'd spoken to the policeman? Was he coming to punish me for what I'd done? Why was he here?

My mind was racing and my stomach turned as he continued to walk across the playground. I wanted to hide, hoping he hadn't seen me. Amongst all the chaos of the other children playing, I began to feel my heart racing, and before I knew what I was doing I was sprinting back into school towards the first teacher I came across. Tears sprung to my eyes as I tried to spit my words out.

The teacher lowered herself onto her knees, grabbing my hand and asking over and over what the matter was. I was screaming inside, yet my tears and fright could not sound the words.

"He's here, please help me!" I cried.

"Who's here?"

"Greg! He's here, and I don't want to go with him!"

She continued to hold my hand as she escorted me to the office, where she instructed me to wait.

I sat there nervously, my whole body shaking uncontrollably as if it were crumbling away to pieces. Moments later, Sarah was brought into the office, making me panic – were they rounding us up to take us back to him?

"It's alright, you're not going home," the teacher told us, "it turns out he's come to get George from school as he has a doctor's appointment later today."

Relieved, I wiped the tears from my face, trying to get my breathing under control again. I'd forgotten this feeling, this effect he had on me, and I vowed from then on that I'd avoid anything in my path that reminded me of him.

It would soon be the summer holidays, which meant it wasn't long before Sarah was to turn nine, and Sylvia had organised for all her friends to come over for a tea party. It was exciting – I couldn't remember any of our previous birthdays, but I sure was going to remember this one.

Sylvia had decorated the big table in the conservatory with balloons and banners and a bright pink tablecloth, matching Sarah's clothes; she wore a bright pink tutu and a black sparkly top, with her hair in pigtails tied with bright pink scrunchies. I knew her endless smile would be imprinted on my mind forever. The table had delicious-looking food spread all over it, with a tall white cake as its centrepiece.

The sun beamed in through the windows as Sarah's friends arrived, and as they gathered around the table to take their seats, Sarah was the centre of attention. She deserved it. I owed her so much – if it hadn't been for her, we would still be with him.

It felt like a long time since Roger and Tanya had paid us a visit, and whenever they came over a sense of uneasiness always arose inside me, knowing they'd have news about our home.

Mummy wanted to see us.

They asked both of us how we felt about this and

whether we wanted to see Mummy. They went on to explain that we would not be going home to see Mummy; it would take place somewhere else, where we'd be watched by either Roger or Tanya.

It was nice to hear that Mummy hadn't forgotten about us – after all, I was sure she loved us both. At times I wondered whether she'd simply been caught within Greg's web and had found it hard to manoeuvre herself away, but none of that seemed to matter now. She wanted to see us, and a part of me felt hope rising slowly up from my gut, feeling that everything was going to be OK.

We were all set for our visit, and soon we found ourselves being driven to this unknown place by Tanya. As I entered what seemed to be a playroom I saw Mummy in the distance, tired and dejected-looking, wilting in a chair.

Passing the colourful books and toys, I swiftly walked towards Mummy, my eyes fixed on her frail face. I felt sorry for her. She sat on the edge of a wooden chair, her legs crossed and her hands placed carefully in her lap, clasped tightly together like a nervous child about to be told off. Her head dropped towards her chin, then lifted when she noticed both Sarah and me approaching. She stood up, shaking like a leaf, as I opened my arms to hug her.

"How are you girls? Oh, I've missed you!" A

creased smile splintered from her mouth as I peered up from my hug to respond.

"We're OK, Mummy," I said. "How's George?"

"Oh, George is fine – the same as usual – and he misses you too."

That afternoon was different from all the other days we'd spent with Mummy. I didn't care much for the books and toys that were scattered about the place; Mummy had my whole attention, and for the first time in what felt like forever, we had hers.

After what seemed like very little time, Tanya politely told us it was time to go.

Saying our goodbyes was hard, Mummy's eyes teary as she said, "Goodbye, and please remember that I love you both dearly." She got up and fell on her knees, wrapping us both in her embrace.

I grabbed Mummy tightly to let her know I still loved her too, and the tears started streaming down Mummy's face. Her eyes glistened and she bent her head down as she slowly placed herself back onto the wooden chair whilst me and Sarah walked out of the room.

Not a word was spoken between us as we drove back to Sylvia and Gordon's house. I was thankful that at least we weren't having to go home to Greg; as much as I missed Mummy and George, I couldn't bear another day with him. Living with Sylvia, I had come to realise that the way he'd treated us was wrong – living in fear each day and not wanting to come home was wrong, yet Mummy knew this. She'd known it all along.

That evening, Sarah seemed dreary as we got unchanged and climbed into bed. I stumbled into the top bunk while Sarah placed herself underneath me on the bottom.

"What's the matter, Sarah?" I asked. "You've been quiet all day."

"I miss Mummy," she replied, "and I want to go home to her." Her words were so quietly spoken and clearly true to how she felt, but I knew I had to try and put a stop to this.

"You can't go back there, Sarah, you can't go back to him. I don't want to go, and that means we'd be split up, and I really don't want that to happen," I said, trying to console her without sounding demanding.

"I don't care about him; Mummy was sad today and she misses us. I would suffer his punishments just to be with Mummy."

"Sarah," I said softly, "think of all the bad stuff he's done to us, but try not to think about it now. Go to sleep. You should feel better in the morning."

I was worried. I was happy where we were, and I certainly didn't want to go back to him – not for anyone.

The next morning, Sylvia and Gordon had a surprise for us: we were going on holiday to Cornwall in a caravan. I had never been on holiday before and I wasn't quite sure what to expect. Feelings of excitement jumped around inside me, my heart pounding fast as I was told to go and pack.

The drive down to Cornwall seemed to take forever, the motorway monotonous as it stretched on for miles and miles. To occupy ourselves we would first spot how many red cars passed us, then lorries and white vans. We played 'I spy with my little eye', although we agreed the answers would have to be something we could actually see, which limited us to either items in the car or what we could see on the endless motorway, such as the lighting.

I could tell we were almost there by the endless fields and mountains I could see in the distance. We were no longer on the motorway; the long stretch of road had turned into muddy country lanes that were bumpy due to the uneven surface.

We soon arrived in a field where there were other campervans, caravans, and tents all set up. Kids were playing in the middle of the field with a ball, throwing it high into the air ready to be caught. The kites caught my eye as they fluttered high into the sky. I couldn't wait to get out of the car and explore the games the other girls and boys were playing.

"Not so fast!" Gordon chirped as I flung open the car door, not thinking to close it as I started making my way to the middle of the field. He wanted us to unpack and to help get the caravan set up before we went off to play.

"Leave them be, Gordon," said Sylvia, "I'm sure you and I have got this – let them play."

My eyes lit up and I glanced at Sarah to share this moment with her. She was already looking at me with a grin as wide as the field we stood in.

We immediately joined the other children, who shared their balls and even their kites with us. I didn't look back at the caravan even once until we were called back for dinner.

"Ahh!" I moaned. I was having so much fun. I could have stayed playing in that very spot for the rest of the time we were there, never imagining all the wonderful things we were going to experience on our holiday, every day packed with adventure.

"This looks delicious," I said. I had never seen a scone filled with jam and whipped cream before and I couldn't wait to get my teeth into it. The cream instantly melted in my mouth and I knew I had managed to get the cream everywhere on my face; after looking at Sarah, who even had cream on her nose, I was sure I did too.

Sylvia and Gordon took us to see the caves, where

it was cold, dark, and wet. I didn't care to stay there for too long as the enclosure of the caves made me feel uneasy.

The beach, on the other hand – oh, how I loved the beach! The waves were high and both me and Sarah would hold hands as we stood waist-deep, jumping over the waves as high as we could.

Sylvia took us crab hunting in between the rock pools, leaving Gordon to have a snooze on the sunbed. I found the crabs to be strange creatures with the way they walked. I would sit and watch as a crab walked sideways to get itself from the water onto the rock.

I was careful not to touch them, though, for fear of getting bitten.

CHAPTER ELEVEN

DECISIONS

IT WAS SOON time to make the dreaded journey back home, yet it seemed to take a lot less time to get home than it did to get there – though that may have been because I fell asleep. Gordon thought it best if we travelled home at night.

I had become accustomed to their house and now saw their house as my own. I hadn't given much thought to Mummy and didn't wonder what she was doing either, until the day when Sylvia had shouted us in from the garden. Roger and Tanya were there.

We were asked to sit as they explained that Daddy had been contacted and he wanted to see us. They explained that we might have to make big decisions about where we would eventually want to live, and that Daddy wanted us to go and live with him. The choices given were Daddy, possibly Mummy, or a new family altogether. I soaked in the information – though I wasn't sure at what point they wanted this decision – but it was clear to me that Sarah was going to choose Mummy.

I tightened my face and gave Sarah a deep probing glance. "No, Sarah, why do you want to go back to Mummy? I don't want to go back to Mummy's and be with him, and I don't want to be split up from you either," I said, taunting her and making sure it was clear what I wanted to do.

"I miss Mummy, that's all," she said, "and George."

"Well, why don't we visit Daddy a few times and see how that goes first?" I urged, hoping this would stall her on her decision.

Sarah agreed, and it wasn't long before we had our first visit with Daddy.

Daddy had a new house with Angela and he showed us around happily, though the house was small and I wondered where he was going to put us as he only had two bedrooms. Daddy explained that he was going to build an extension from the kitchen so that we'd have a brand new bedroom with a toilet off the side.

We visited Daddy's house several times over the

following months. I enjoyed my visits and began to feel like it could be my home. Angela was always welcoming, and her son Matthew was very chirpy, making it almost feel like he'd replaced the brother we once had.

It was soon time to start high school, so Sylvia arranged a visit with the local high school not far from home. I was growing up, I thought to myself as I entered the classrooms, which were much bigger than I was used to. Sylvia told me I would soon make friends – she must have seen the worried look on my face – and she was right, as I started to get after-school invites from friends to come around for tea.

One day, as I made my way upstairs to get changed out of my uniform, Sylvia called both me and Sarah downstairs. "Your Mummy's on the phone, do you want to speak to her?" she asked politely, though I could see she wasn't happy about it.

I picked up the phone and, sure enough, Mummy was on the other end. "Hello Mummy," I said shyly, having not spoken to her in such a long time.

"Hello Kelly. I can't stay on the phone for too long as I'm calling from America."

"Oh," I replied, confused as to why she would be in America. I had no idea where America was, but I knew you had to get on a plane to get there, and that it was far away.

"I'm going to be living here now, Kelly, but I'd like to stay in touch with you, and call you from time to time, if that's OK?"

My eyes widened with shock. I was speechless. I didn't really know what to say, so all I could reply with was, "Yes, OK." I had so many questions I wanted to ask, but Sarah was clinging to me, staring at me to pass her the phone.

I immediately handed the phone over to Sarah; Mummy had explained that she had to be quick with her call and I sensed the quickness in her tone. I then hurried back upstairs so I wouldn't have to explain this to Sylvia, but who was I kidding? She probably already knew, and that was why she wasn't happy about the phone call. I knew Sarah was going to be upset, and that it would possibly destroy her, what with her expressions of wanting to go back to live with Mummy. I knew this wouldn't be possible now, leaving us with no choice but to go and live with Daddy. I was angry at Mummy, but I knew Sarah would forgive her for anything, even running off to America with him.

Images flashed through my mind, taking me back to when we lived in Germany with Daddy and Mummy. I saw us playing in the back garden having our barbecues, laughing and happy. It seemed like a million years ago.

I gazed up at the sky from my bedroom window, to consider whether God was there, if he was listening. Would he assist in lifting my load of worry that usually hindered me? Mummy had gone, leaving two children behind, would she be sorry for the future she had now written for herself. Was this Gods plan for her, for me, for Sarah? So many unanswered questions that lurked deep in my mind.

It was time to do some housework at home and I knew I would never do this as well as Sarah, which often made Sylvia disappointed. Having been given the task of cleaning the bathroom I would strut about the house, making it well known in my performance that I wasn't happy. I hated housework as it reminded me of him, and I vowed that I would never do it again, yet as I sat and pondered over this, I knew deep down that as I got older, I would have to clean. It wasn't something I could avoid for the rest of my life, but for now I was happy with my moaning and my performance, and with letting Sarah get all the credit for doing a better job than I. It was easier for me to escape the full horror of my past situation by not talking about it.

Time moved on swiftly as I got used to my new school and made new friends. I was given the freedom to ride my bike to the park and was even allowed to go to the shops with my friends by myself. This was a whole new me.

I no longer feared being punished in the way Greg used to punish us, yet whenever someone was close to me and moved their arms or legs within my personal space, I couldn't help but flinch. My eyes would close so tight that I was sure the whole of my face wrinkled and my nose creased, waiting for the blow across my face that never came. No matter how hard I tried I simply couldn't stop it, this trait I hadn't noticed before.

The time soon came when we had to say our good-byes to Sylvia and Gordon so we could go and live with our daddy. With each visit to Daddy we had seen the development of our new bedroom coming along, and Daddy and Angela had even taken us shopping to pick out our new bedroom furniture. Our beds were grey and we both had a matching desk and chair to sit on so we could do our homework. I helped Angela paint the walls a cream colour and, once this was dry, she nailed notice boards and pictures on the wall to give the room some colour. I liked it. It was ours.

CHAPTER TWELVE

NEW BEGINNINGS?

THIS WAS OUR new home, and before long we were introduced to our new schools. I was surprised as it was an all-girls school – not one single boy in sight – while Sarah's school was next to mine, as she wasn't quite ready to go to big school yet. My uniform stood out as it was green (not a colour I would have chosen for girls) but looking on the bright side I was sure to make friends with the vast amount of girls that went there.

My first day at school was memorable as I was introduced to Mrs Burnett, a fierce history teacher. Her hair was extremely curly and blonde, and she presented as tall and slightly bigger in weight, though she dressed exquisitely, proud almost in who she was, which showed in her clothing.

That first day, Mrs Burnett gathered all the girls into a room for a meeting to discuss how the year was progressing – and to discuss bodily hygiene.

"Now, girls, we all know about periods and why we get them," she roared at us, "but it has come to my attention that not everyone changes their sanitary pads often enough. What happens when we don't do that?"

Oh my, I thought – I hadn't even started mine yet and I blushed at the thought that I would soon have to deal with this, and that I'd have to talk to someone about it.

"Yes, Mrs Burnett," everyone had answered in harmony – everyone except me.

"Blood begins to smell as it rots away, girls, and if you don't change your pad after you've been running around then other people begin to notice." She went on to explain about uniforms and keeping ourselves tidy, as well as reminding us that trainers must not be worn, and then she said – quite sternly – that if anyone was sent to her office after this talk, detention would be set.

Everyone feared Mrs Burnett whenever she walked down the corridors of the school. Her walk was always distinctive; she wore high heels and she went at a slow pace, as if to take in every inch of us as she passed. Yet although her tone was stern, her bright blue eyes told another story – one of kindness and fairness.

I sat in her history class ensuring that I didn't make myself known – as I didn't want to get into any trouble – and as I leant my head down towards my workbook to write, I could hear her walking towards me, her heels clicking loudly on the floor.

Bending over my desk, she introduced herself and asked me to do the same.

Well, I knew quite clearly from all the other children – and from the meeting in the hall – who she was, and I was surprised that out of all the children she had taken the time to spot I was new. From that moment on I knew I could approach her with anything, and as the weeks went on, I found myself standing outside her office to have chats with her about my life.

It was soon announced by Daddy and the new social worker that I was to attend counselling for an hour each week during school time. The new social worker hadn't been with us long and didn't feel it necessary to come to our new home anymore to check up on me and Sarah.

I attended my counselling sessions as I was asked, though some days I just sat in silence as I stared at this unfamiliar woman sitting opposite me. But, as time passed, I began to talk about all the cruel and nasty things Greg had done to us. I wasn't sure about the benefits of this as I never got any response back, just tape recordings – I watched the counsellor place the tapes in and out of the cassette player. I much preferred to talk to Mrs Burnett.

A year had nearly passed since we'd started living with Daddy, and things had begun to change. Sarah was entering high school herself and there were tensions at home between Daddy and Angela. I had arrived home from school that day to notice a familiar pacing back and forth from the kitchen to the living room. I had witnessed my Mummy doing that years and years ago, and now Angela was doing it too. I looked intently at her pale face and the frown that stretched wide across her forehead, which deterred me from asking what was wrong.

I hurried to my bedroom, where Sarah had already beaten me home, and asked if she knew what was going on.

"No," she sighed with a look of disappointment in her eyes. Neither of us wanted any discomfort in the house.

When Angela called us for tea, I noticed that Daddy wasn't home from work. He was usually home by teatime, and even though I wondered about it I was still scared to ask for fear that I'd add further frowns to the ones Angela already had on her face.

We sat through most of our tea in silence, bringing back memories of feeling alone at Mummy's when I would sit alone, left to ponder my own deep, dark thoughts.

The silence was eventually broken by Angela, asking us to get ready for bed and to go and retire to our room. I did as I was told; I found comfort in my room, even though I shared it with Sarah. This was my one safe place, as no bad memories had entered this room. There was no past within these walls, just the present, and dreams of the future.

I lay my head on my pillow whilst I spoke to Sarah about my day and asked her about hers. "Have you met Mrs Burnett yet, Sarah?" I asked with a giggle, awaiting her response.

"Yes, she looks scary," she replied. "On my first day she gathered us all into the hall and spoke to us about our uniforms and how we should act and treat others."

I could hear the nervousness in her voice, which only enhanced my laughter further. "Mrs Burnett is nice, Sarah – you just have to speak to her, you'll see."

I must have drifted off to sleep in the midst of speaking to Sarah because before I knew it, I was being woken by Angela in the middle of the night, demanding that me and Sarah get out of bed.

I did as I was told, following Angela into the dark living room, where she yelled from the bottom of the stairs up to Daddy. "Now your girls can see what you're really like!"

Daddy's home, I thought, wondering what could have happened to make Angela so mad.

Daddy appeared at the top of the stairs, where he seemed to stumble, leaning against the wall that somehow supported his weight. I stood staring aimlessly at him above, waiting for a response that never came. He just waved his hand up and back and forth – as if to summon us to go away – and then wandered back into his bedroom.

I wasn't sure why Angela had woken us, but she too turned on her heel and ordered us back into the living room. "Go and get your blankets," she said, "we'll sleep in the living room for the rest of the night."

I was confused as I lay my blanket out on the couch for me and Sarah, then curled my body around her to stay warm. Once she'd settled, Sarah turned to grin at me, her eyes already tired, whispering goodnight.

I, on the other hand, became restless, staring up at the ceiling and sensing the great silence of the house. I listened for Daddy but heard not a whisper of any movement coming from upstairs – not from Matthew, who continued to sleep, not from Daddy, and not even from a car passing by outside.

The following morning I dragged myself off the couch, and oh boy, was I tired. I was still none the wiser as to why Angela was angry, but that didn't matter now as I had to get ready for school.

The day seemed to drag through the yawns, my eyes teasing me to close them halfway through the day, and by home time I could feel my temper rising as all I wanted to do was go to bed.

I felt annoyed with Angela, and when we got home and she asked if I had any homework, I snapped back, "No!" I wanted to sleep, not do homework.

She stared at me in an odd, harassed way and growled, "Don't speak to me like that, young lady!"

"You're not my mum so you can't tell me what to do!" I shot back, and in that instant, I thought she might slap me. I'd realised what I'd said and could not take it back.

In response she grounded me for a whole week and made me walk to school every day.

Resentment was starting to kick in on a daily basis, as Angela had taken over the ruling of me and Sarah and my daddy was hardly to be seen. My anguish grew and grew, soon turning to a mountain of rage. We were no longer allowed to sit in the living room to watch television with Daddy, Angela, and Matthew, although we were allowed in the back room to watch it – me and Sarah would sit together and watch our favourite show, *Little House on the Prairie.*

Our weekends had become packed with dance lessons that Angela had organised for us to attend, with ballet, tap and modern on a Friday and Saturday morning. I loved dancing. Dancing would centre my mind on focusing on the steps, rather than anything else in my life. I would momentarily forget my thoughts of Mummy, Daddy, and life in general, dancing until I was out of breath and picking myself up whenever I fell after doing a pirouette. My leotard glued to me from the sweat as I imagined dancing in front of thousands of people, people who noticed and liked me. Me, who glided along the stage rather than gliding through life. I would dream of becoming a brilliant dancer when I was older, when I would marry and settle down to have lots of beautiful children. Although I didn't know what kind of man I would marry, I knew that he would have to be brilliant. He would have to want children and have a future; he would have to measure up to the daddy I once knew.

A year had gone by when Mummy called the house phone again to talk to me and Sarah. Mummy always seemed to have this shy, timid voice when she spoke to us – even when she announced that she was coming to England to see us.

"When are you coming, Mummy? I can't wait to

see you!" I screeched in excitement. I missed Mummy – just being around her and being able to talk to her.

"I'm coming next week," she replied. "Daddy knows all about it, and we'll be staying at Nanny and Grandad's house for a couple of weeks."

That soon? I thought to myself happily. I couldn't wait to see everyone – it felt like such a long time since I'd seen the rest of my family.

Both me and Sarah came away from the phone excited, only for that to evaporate as soon as we heard Angela and Daddy arguing over Mummy's visit. Daddy had agreed for us to stay with Mummy for the whole two weeks, yet Angela wasn't happy as my Daddy's father was coming for a short break and Angela felt it important that we were here to see him.

My eyes widened further. Were we not going to get to see Mummy? I didn't know much about my grandad from Daddy's side of the family, but in that moment I couldn't help but feel annoyed. We could see Grandad anytime, but Mummy was now living thousands of miles away and I didn't know when we'd be able to see her again.

Eventually Daddy had given in to the argument and agreed that we'd only spend a week with Mummy instead of two, which was just so unfair. I stomped about like the school child I was, pulling faces at Angela at every opportunity and ignoring her whenever possible, until Daddy told me, "That's enough!"

He was right, of course, because my stubbornness didn't get me any further. So, I convinced myself that it really didn't matter if we didn't get to spend the whole two weeks with her. We still had the one.

Soon, it was time to see Mummy. Excited, I had packed a few items of clothing and made sure I had all my necessities ready for the week ahead. Mummy had called once she'd arrived at Nanny's house, this time with excitement in her voice, not the shy, timid woman I had become accustomed to hearing. It was torture knowing that she was already in the country and had to spend her first week without us whilst we stayed and entertained Grandad. Yet, sure enough, that week skipped by so fast that the time soon came when Daddy was yelling at me from the car to hurry up.

"I'm coming!" I yelled back.

The drive to Aldershot was short – not long, like I imagined –and then there it was: the bungalow I had so missed and dreamt of for many a night.

I didn't wait for Daddy to give me permission as he parked his car on the driveway; I couldn't wait to get the door open and fling myself out. Then, racing to the side door, I stopped in my tracks as a wave of anxiety suddenly hit me right in the chest.

I realised that I hadn't seen Mummy for nearly two years. What if she didn't like the way I looked, or how I was, or *who* I was? Just as all these soaring thoughts come racing to me, the door opened and out came Mummy, Nanny, and Grandad.

My legs began to shake as I watched Sarah immediately run over and grasp her in her arms. I observed the whole thing intently as the overwhelming feeling that she was here hit me.

I studied Mummy closely. Her hair was shorter than it used to be, and blonder, and she seemed to have shrunk a little since the last time I'd seen her. She walked – still with Sarah in her arms –towards me and stretched out her other arm to grab me and pull me in for a huge hug. I was only too delighted to hug her back.

"Let's get inside and I'll put the kettle on," Nanny announced.

There was too much going on outside, with Mummy hurriedly talking to us to get all her news in as if we only had a matter of moments, and Grandad and Daddy discussing the scarce traffic on the drive over here.

Inside it felt very familiar; nothing had changed in the kitchen since the last time I'd been there, and not a thing was out of place. Grandad was also still the same – it was like we'd never gone. I always thought that Grandad spoilt us a little, even with his gestures and the time he took to make me laugh.

Mummy was happy. It had been a long time since I'd seen an unceasing smile on her face, which she had now as she expressed how much she'd missed us both and didn't want to let us go. It was a different Mummy than I'd been so used to over the past few years.

The next few days flew by. We spent most of our time lounging about, talking and giggling, and taking nice country walks. Daddy even showed up on one of the nights and took Mummy out for a drink. They must have had plenty to talk about, as I watched the hands of the clock go around several times while I waited for Mummy to return. We even went to see Auntie Caroline, who had her own place with Uncle Graham – she always opened her arms to me and Sarah.

One day, Mummy called Greg to let him know that she was OK and to check on George. It suddenly dawned on me that I hadn't asked about George at all, and in that moment all my burning questions came rushing out.

"What is George doing, Mummy? Is he going to school? Does he have friends? Does he miss me and Sarah?"

"Slow down, Kelly," she laughed, "and the answer is yes to all those questions."

We sat for a while discussing Mummy's life in America. She explained that it was difficult living there and that she couldn't work for the first year she was out there. She didn't want to go back, I could sense that, but I also knew that she had to as George was there, and he couldn't be left all by himself.

The week ended and Daddy arrived to take us home. Tears were falling in all directions as we said our goodbyes. Mummy was sad, which made me sad, feeling helpless and sorry that she had to go back to America.

When we returned home, I deeply expressed that I wanted to spend more time at Auntie Caroline's house. I had felt safe and secure there and she listened to me. Mummy had returned to America and had called us to let us know she was safe. I began to cry as Mummy expressed that if we'd asked her to, she would have stayed in England and would not have returned. I was tortured by this as I had no idea that she wanted us to ask her, and if I'd known, I would definitely have asked her to stay.

Not thinking about George being left there all alone, I asked her while she was on the phone, begging her to come back, but she told me she didn't have enough money now to make it back to England again – it was too late.

That night (and for continuous nights ahead) I

fretted in and out of sleep, tormented and restless, and feeling angry, helpless, and frustrated at myself that I didn't ask her to stay while she was still here.

Fortunately, Daddy promised that I could go and stay with Auntie Caroline whenever it was possible. She lived in Aldershot too, in an army house with my Uncle Graham, and I felt at home with her. By now Daniel had arrived – my cousin, cute and adorable – and even though Auntie Caroline was busy seeing to Daniel, she never had any less time for me.

I had always admired Auntie Caroline's curly hair, so one day I asked her how I could get my hair curly like hers.

"Come on," she said.

"Why, where are we going?" I asked, slightly concerned that I was in trouble.

"To get your hair done! Let's make it curly."

Feeling optimistic, I sprang to my feet and followed her to the car, where she took me to the hairdressers. I was to get a perm, and after what felt like hours my hair was finally done. It was positively worth the wait; I couldn't believe my eyes, and I also couldn't believe she would do this for me, without a second thought.

When I arrived back home, Angela wasn't impressed with what I'd done to my hair. "You didn't even ask permission to get this done, Kelly," she said, angry.

I was annoyed. Why would I need to ask her permission when I was with my auntie? Surely Auntie Caroline had more rights over me than she did – at least she was actual family.

Angela's eyes looked bleak as she looked my hair up and down.

A bitter and twisted emotion trampled through my brain, there was no reasoning with her as my courage to fight back drained from every inch of my body, fixated, she seemed an outsider to me now - this was not the Angela who'd once spoken to us only with kindness and love. Back to my hair her eyes skipped, then she deliberately turned her back on me. She ordered me to immediately go and wash my hair, to wash the curls out. I didn't understand.

I felt the squeezing of my blood sucked dry from my tiny body as I stomped up the stairs towards the bathroom. I swore, using words I'd never used before. For once I had felt pretty, and whenever I was around Auntie Caroline she made me feel important. With her, I acted my age and held my poise. Yet here I felt I had a fake house, fake parents, and a fake life.

A couple of years had gone by and with each year that passed, when the summer was upon us, I got to see Mummy. I went to stay with Auntie Caroline regularly too. I was growing, developing into a woman at the age of fourteen, and for the first time my menstrual cycle was upon me. I relished in my womanliness, though thoughts of Mrs Burnett's past words, became the forefront of my mind.

The cramping hurt and never had I seen so much blood or felt so much discomfort, just so that one day I could bear a child. On months like this, I still pined for Mummy. So, whenever Mummy would come to visit, Sarah and I would spend the whole two weeks begging her to stay. The relentless begging never worked, however, because each time she would return to America. I still didn't understand – I thought this was what she wanted, for us to ask her to stay.

It was time now to start exploring Daddy's side of the family. Angela had told us that we were going to stay with our Auntie Margaret and Uncle Steve for a while in Doncaster, and there we also had three cousins: Lucy, Johnathan, and Thomas.

I couldn't wait to get there as we drove for hours on a mindless motorway that offered no stimulation or view of any kind. When we arrived I thought the houses looked like London townhouses, some with alleyways to get access to the back gardens.

After carrying our bags over, Daddy knocked on the door and Margaret answered. She looked like Daddy, only she was bigger. Her hair was brown, short at the sides and spiky on the top.

"Hello, how was the drive?" she asked as she directed us into the house.

Just as we were invited to settle ourselves on the living room chairs, I could hear the stairs thumping as heavy feet came running down. It was Johnathan and Thomas. Auntie Margaret had already explained that Lucy was out babysitting – she was a lot older than me and Sarah and had responsibilities – so we would get to meet her later.

Johnathan took little interest in us; he was tall and blond and older too; he was, however, polite to us both and introduced himself, asking us how our journey was. Then, to my surprise, in came Thomas – tall, dark, and handsome, with a cheeky smile. A rippling sensation on the back of my neck made me aware that he was there, and I stood trembling, weak, perplexed, and dazed while he walked slowly towards me. I could feel my eyes flickering, my face flushing as his eyes lowered from my face down to my feet and then travelled back up, ever so slowly. Then he spoke; he introduced himself and placed himself down onto a seat.

Still blushing, I couldn't find my tongue to respond back, and for the first time I felt embarrassed and ashamed, yet his eyes and his look made me come alive.

When it was time for Daddy to leave and go back

home, I became excited at the prospect of staying there again, especially when we were shown to our room that we'd share with Lucy for the next week. Auntie Margaret and Uncle Steve had to continue to go to work while we visited. Margaret was a bus driver and explained that she still had to carry out her duties so that everyone could get to work, and Steve was a lorry driver. To my delight, Thomas had arranged to take us out to the cinema and the ice skating rink during the week.

The next day we went skating; Thomas escorted us onto the bus and away we went. I was grown up by now – or, at least, it felt like I was grown up – and his charming yet reckless behaviour intrigued me.

Placing the skates on my feet, I suddenly realised I couldn't skate. I'd never been skating before and hadn't known how cold this place would be.

Thomas carefully placed his hand upon mine to help me stand, and I willingly clasped hold of his hand as I followed him onto the ice. He was a good skater – I could tell he must do it regularly. I, on the other hand, glided around the best I could – that was, until Thomas let go, thinking it was funny to leave me.

"Thomas, where are you going?" I called out into the distance, hoping with every breath that I wouldn't fall to the ground, much to my embarrassment.

Trying to concentrate, I headed towards the wall

to steady myself as the music played on. There was no sign of Thomas. Then, suddenly, he approached me, wrapping his long arms around me to steady me further. This contact sent ripples down my spine and caused me to blush; I had never experienced any form of touch like this from a boy before.

As quickly as he'd grabbed me, he was off again, and a second later my knees gave way and I fell forward, right onto the ice.

Thomas's face hovered over mine, and he reached his hand out to help pull me up from the ground. His usually playful eyes looked worried and intense, sparkling against the light as he asked if I was OK.

A lump came into my throat as I wondered why I felt this way towards my cousin – just that look of his held me in thrall. "I'm OK," I choked.

We skated hand in hand for the rest of our stay until it was time to go home.

We talked about everything that afternoon, though Thomas mostly boasted about all the bad stuff he got up to, including expressing that he was a better driver than my daddy.

"How can you be? You're not old enough to drive," I chuckled at him, not realising that he was known for getting himself into trouble.

His hands raised to disguise the mood of his face, and when he lowered his armour to come out from behind his shield, he looked amused. Clearing his throat, he said, "Come on, it's time for bed. I'll take you to the cinema tomorrow to watch *Beethoven*."

After all the excitement I'd had today, I couldn't wait until tomorrow, wondering what it would bring.

Back at the house, I lay my head on my pillow, excited to see the film yet also excited to see him. I knew it was wrong, yet this overwhelming feeling that I had to be near him took hold of me completely. For the first time in my life I was overwhelmed with this warm feeling of wanting to give my own love. I closed my eyes, picturing and reminiscing about the day that had just occurred, until I eventually fell asleep.

The next morning I sprung from bed, eager to get going, then headed to the bathroom to make myself lovely for the day ahead. Helping myself to breakfast, I asked Lisa where Thomas was. It appeared that he was already up, dressed, and out. He was an early bird and always had ants in his pants and therefore couldn't stay in one place for too long, which always got him into trouble, or so I was told.

"Oh," I sighed in disappointment, hoping he hadn't forgotten about taking me to the cinema today.

Once the dishes were washed from breakfast, I placed myself in the living room to watch television just in time to hear the back door go. I hoped it would be Thomas and it was.

"Are you ready?" he asked with a mischievous smile that would break anyone's heart.

I shot up, grabbed my coat, and followed him out of the house. I was quiet through most of the journey, embarrassed and worried that he could read my thoughts – that he'd know I'd carefully pondered every step he and I made yesterday, so as not to make the same mistakes of falling over again.

The cinema was half full, and on entering the room where the film was to be shown Thomas grabbed my hand without permission and led me to the very back row. This film is going to be good, I thought to myself, and even more so with him sitting next to me. I felt guarded and protected in a way no man or boy had ever made me feel before. This was a completely new experience.

I continued to watch the film, though I was only half paying attention to it as Thomas was still holding my hand. My heart began to pound faster, wondering if he was aware that the palms of my hands had started to become sweaty. Oh no, I thought, surely he's going to let go in a minute – how could anyone be attracted to the warm dampness of a clammy hand? And with that he repositioned our hands, sliding his fingers into mine so the cool breeze of air could cool down our palms.

The film was good, and as we caught the bus

home we discussed the film in detail while laughing and joking, all the while still holding hands.

Back at his house, we realised that everyone had gone out and we were alone. I ran upstairs to change my top, conscious that I had overheated at times in the cinema. When I turned to come out of the room I found him standing there in the doorway.

He calmly walked towards me as I stood there nervously, my heart pounding with uncertainty about what was going to happen.

He embraced me, placing his arm around my back and pushing me against the bedroom wall. He then whispered in my ear, asking me if I was OK. I responded yes, my chest pounding – leaping, dipping, and fluttering – sure that he'd be able to feel it. He clung to me more tightly, knotting his other hand in my hair, his soft eyes staring straight into mine as he pressed his warm lips upon mine.

I was deep into the thrusting of his mouth when he gently moved his hand from my hair, brushing his fingertips softly against my breasts. I didn't object. He continued to explore my hot flesh, stroking my bare tummy as he lifted my top off over my head. As his lips began to explore my cheek and then my neck, he was like a raging fire that couldn't be tamed.

He unbuttoned my trousers, leaving me to feel raw and exposed, then continued to press his lips against my open flesh, making his way down to my tummy as he knelt. He slipped off my trousers, leaving me feeling vulnerable. If it wasn't for his eyes that burnt upon mine I may have crumbled, wanting to cover up my nakedness.

Taking hold of my hand, he led me to the bed, leaving me lusting for more as I shyly watched him get undressed. He placed his body on mine, so satisfying in every way, and then he filled me, entering me gently.

Sweat formed on his forehead as he quickened his tempo, getting progressively faster with a vigorous intensity. Then he arched his back, rising and falling and calling out my name in satisfaction.

Catching his breath, he fell to one side of me, resuming the caressing of my skin with his finger. I was in love in that very moment – on fire – yet most of all I felt desired.

The couple of days we had left together were filled with sneaking passionate kisses at every given opportunity, leaving me pining for more. I lusted for more every time I felt the warmth of his tongue beneath mine. We were scarcely alone, and I wanted to scream out and be near him all the time, even though I knew this was forbidden.

When it was time to go home, I knew I had to carry this forbidden secret with me. I pined for the rest of the summer, not knowing what to do with myself or who to turn to as I had no way of contacting him. I sat and wondered whether he felt the same or whether this was just a notch on his bedpost. My wandering around the house like a lost puppy was soon noticed by Daddy, and he eventually came and asked me what the matter was.

"Kelly, you've been wandering around with a sad look on your face for two weeks now, what is the matter?" he asked, as if it was his duty to find out.

I wondered whether it was Angela who had instructed him to come and talk to me. Either way, I decided in that moment that I needed to share my secret with him in the hope that he'd be able to help me and come to my rescue. So, I went on to explain what had happened between Thomas and I, and that I missed him dearly and had never felt like this before.

I didn't even have a chance to finish before I saw Daddy's face drop, pale from the shock. The look of disappointment in his eyes struck me, before they quickly became overridden with anger. Immediately after my words were out, I wanted to take them back. I was drowning in shame.

He stood so that he hung over me, forbidding me to ever see Thomas again and saying that he never imagined it would be this that I had to tell him.

For the first time in a while, I felt the cold tears

start to fall down my face. I knew what I'd done was wrong, but I never imagined that he'd feel this way towards me.

Dad looked at me, not with admiration or pride but only with pity – and to reprimand me, for it was weeks before he started talking to me again. In the meantime, he made me feel as though I was excluded from the household, yet I didn't care; I had become hardened to it, and had decided that I'd find my own way to contact Thomas.

As soon as school started again, I phoned Thomas's house from a phone box and, to my surprise, he answered.

"I miss you," I explained, though I wasn't to worry as he said he would travel to London that very weekend with a couple of his friends and that he'd come and see me. I knew this couldn't happen at Dad's house so I planned to stay at a friend's house, where we could sneak out at night to go and meet him.

That evening I felt thrills run down my spine, and overridden with excitement, I could hardly contain myself. My school friend was more than willing to participate in my shenanigans, as her parents were a lot less strict than mine.

At my friend's house, I pruned myself until I was ready and then pretended to put myself to bed. After a couple of hours of silence, we climbed out of the bedroom window and made our way down to the canal – where we were to meet him – and, sure enough, he was there. Walking over to him, I leaped into his arms.

He grabbed me tight and began to caress my cheeks, my body humming at the recollection of his previous touch as he pressed his lips against mine. He fiercely rubbed his hands down my back, all the way down to my buttocks and back up again, clutching both hands in my hair before letting go. I stared at him wide-eyed, feeling the rush of his kiss as he explained that he had to go and couldn't stay.

My disappointment whooshed right through me, my excitement coming to a sudden halt as he left just as quickly as he'd arrived. I felt so angry – all this heartache, and for what?

We slowly walked back to my friend's house, quietly sneaking back in, where her parents awaited us. I knew we were in trouble and that I'd have a lot of explaining to do to Angela when I returned home the following morning.

Angela stood coldly as I entered the house, staring at me with eyes full of disappointment. My own disappointment came rushing back too, as I felt I'd been denied the one person I had grown to care about. Her voice was stern as she informed me I would be grounded and would no longer be able to stay over at a friend's house. She also went on to explain that the whole family knew about me and Thomas and were not best pleased.

I cried through most of that day, coming to the realisation that I would probably never see him again. Why hadn't he stayed that night? Did he not want to be with me? What was wrong with me?

I plodded along at school, while my friends teased me about how mischievous I'd been – especially as I wasn't normally one for getting into trouble.

Dad had arranged for me and Sarah to go and spend some time with his brother and his wife, Carl and Sally, who lived in a place called Salisbury just a short drive past Stonehenge. They lived in what seemed like the countryside, with plenty of fields and just a small town, where everybody seemed to know each other. Sally had three children, all younger than myself, so being the oldest, I felt very grown up.

Sally had short blonde hair and a very caring nature; she was always tending to her children and ensuring they were OK. Carl just followed her lead. He had dark brown hair – that he kept rather short to disguise the thinning and loss from on top – and was full of confidence, often preparing barbecues and inviting all the neighbours on the street to attend. After a couple of drinks, however, he would begin to get loud, causing slight disputes between him and

Sally as she accused him of flirting with other women. I only knew this because in one heated discussion she mumbled under her breath that he'd previously had an affair with one of her friends.

After the meal this one evening Sally had retreated to bed just as she'd done previously, exhausted from the day and the heated discussions, to settle the kids into bed and say her goodnights. I found myself left alone with Carl, slumped in his chair with a beer in one hand. After a few moments he opened a discussion up about Thomas and me.

"So, what's the crack with you and Thomas then?" he asked sheepishly so as not to overstep the mark.

I shrugged my shoulders, unsure how to answer his question. To be honest I didn't really want to discuss it; I didn't want all those feelings rushing back or me pining for him for the rest of my stay.

"Well," Carl continued, undeterred by my silence, "I never get any from her; she's always putting herself to bed, and then when I do get some, she just lays there like a sack of potatoes – and she wonders why I go elsewhere!" He said this to me as if I was Sally, staring at me with intense eyes as he waited for me to reply.

Feeling the pressure to respond as he continued to stare at me, I said, "Oh, right, maybe you should speak to her about it then." I didn't really know what to say to him, so I just said whatever sprang to mind.

Taking a swig of his beer, he said, "You are beautiful – has anyone ever told you that before?"

"No, not really," I replied in shock. By now I wanted to get myself to bed, but I felt uncomfortable doing so in fear that he'd think I was rude.

"Bet I could teach you a thing or two," he continued, "not like Thomas – he's just a boy."

"I don't know," I replied. What was he expecting me to say? The palms of my hands started to sweat as an uncomfortable feeling washed over me – the kind of feeling I hadn't felt since being with Mummy.

How did he know what I'd done with Thomas? Oh gosh, did *everyone* know?

I stood up then, announcing that I was going to bed. Carl didn't respond; he just sat there, continuing to drink his beer. I was pleased about this, and also pleased that I'd be in the same room as Sarah, in case he tried to enter.

The following morning, I didn't say anything to Sally, coming to the conclusion that Carl had just had too much to drink and probably wouldn't remember what he'd said anyway.

That day, Sally had decided to take us out on a walk. The country was so beautiful, I could have walked for miles. She explained that we were going to go to a festival in the next couple of days – one that the whole community attends – and that me and Sarah would get to meet everyone.

I was excited – I loved music and found solace in listening to it whenever I had the opportunity. "Will there be music playing?" I asked.

"Yes, of course, there always is at a festival."

Oh goody, I thought to myself.

Back at Sally's house she taught me how to cook chilli con carne, but instead of using chilli beans she used baked beans for the children's sake.

"I can't eat anything spicy," I implored. I wouldn't go near any spicy food as it reminded me of Greg, and I feared that I would choke.

"It's OK, I don't put any spices in it because of the children –otherwise they won't eat it!" she chuckled, at the same time giving me my reassurance.

After dinner Sally decided she was going to retire for the night. Carl had been nice all day, so I didn't see the harm in sitting with him to watch some television.

I was wrong.

As the night progressed, he brought up the subject of Thomas again. "Have you given any thought to what I said?" he asked casually.

What was he saying? What did I need to think about? Surely, he knew he shouldn't have spoken to me like that last night, right?

I shook my head vigorously so that he'd understand

I was saying no. In that instant, I regretted not going to bed with Sarah, as now I would have to make my excuses again. "What do you mean?" I responded with a shallow crackle in my voice, hoping that perhaps he may have been talking about something else.

"I've explained to you that I could teach you a thing or two, that you are beautiful, and that Thomas doesn't know what he's missing by letting you go like that."

I grew weary of hearing talk of love; how young and impressionable I was! I was confused, yet he said it in such a way that he made it sound like he cared about me. Why would he be concerned about my feelings towards Thomas, and about what happened?

Then, much to my surprise, he stood, saying he wanted to caress my breasts and relieve himself over me, then asked my permission to do so.

I shook my head in disbelief, yet I felt some pity for him – maybe he was right; maybe Sally did go to bed every night and didn't tend to his needs.

He pleaded with me, telling me he wouldn't hurt me in any way and that I was so beautiful that he could hardly contain himself.

So, I agreed, and began to unbutton my shirt, my fingers trembling. As I reached the last button he helped me take my shirt off, then he pulled me to my feet and asked me to lie on the floor on my back. "Take off your bra," he instructed, demanding yet reassuring with his words.

I lay staring at the ceiling, feeling exposed, and turned my head away so I wouldn't have to watch him pull the top half of his jeans off. He began to caress himself but I didn't look; I closed my eyes, my mind blank, listening to him grunting until I felt this warm substance hit my chest, making me jolt in slight shock.

It was over quickly, and I continued to lay still while he composed himself and wiped down my chest.

Breathless, he said, "Wow, you are good, that didn't take me long at all." He was smiling at me.

I sat up to fumble for my bra, feeling embarrassed that I was still exposed while he was dressed, and he leant down and pulled my face gently towards him until we locked eyes.

"Kelly, you do know that we can't tell Sally what went on here, don't you?"

Speechless, I nodded. Of course I knew I couldn't say anything – she'd be so mad at me for doing this.

"If you say anything, your dad will have me locked away in a prison – and you too, probably – so this will be our little secret."

"OK," I responded, "can I go to bed now?"

"Yes. See you tomorrow, beautiful, and thank you."

Was he really thanking me? At least now he might leave me alone, I supposed, and I knew from that moment onwards I would not stay up with him of an evening; I would go to bed when Sally went to bed.

The following day was the festival. I had summoned myself to forget about the night before, knowing that he wouldn't get to do that again as I would see my plan through and not stay up. I wouldn't let this ruin my day ahead.

It was a short walk to the festival down the country lanes, and we soon came to this massive open field, full of people. It was loud and lively and there was plenty of food to feed the whole community.

We'd just settled at a table when Sally realised she'd forgotten the juice back at the house.

"I'll go back and get it," Carl insisted. "Come on, Kelly, you can help me."

I looked at Sally, who agreed with Carl, and I nervously stood up, my legs wobbling at the thought of being alone with him.

Walking back to the house, Carl started again. "You really aroused me last night, but I feel like I haven't got enough. Would you like me to teach you something else?" he asked.

Inwardly I cringed, my voice turning cold as I replied, "OK." I couldn't really say anything else; I just wanted it over with so I could get back to the festival and enjoy the day.

Back at the house, he grabbed my hands and led me to his bed. "Come on then, pull your pants down – we can't be gone for too long otherwise Sally will wonder where we are."

I hurriedly took my jeans off and lay on the bed as ordered, then he climbed on top of me and entered me. He was thrusting too hard – my stomach started to hurt with the pressure – and before I knew it, he was done.

It didn't feel like this with Thomas, and he hadn't hurt me either. It had felt natural with Thomas, and I wanted to do forbidden things with him, but with Carl I felt pressured; I'd only done this forbidden act to get him off my back.

"Come on, get dressed," he said as he himself got dressed, "we have to go. And remember: not a word to anyone. I'm sure you don't want to see me go to prison, do you?"

It was with reluctance and fear that I shook my head. I didn't want to see anyone go to prison, and I didn't want anyone to be mad at me either.

Back at the festival I stayed quiet as my tummy began to do somersaults, the dull ache piercing me and leaving me clenching my stomach with both hands.

I couldn't concentrate on my surroundings; the

day was ruined, and I began to feel tearful, thinking how I just wanted to go back home to Dad's house and crawl under my duvet.

CHAPTER THIRTEEN

MY FINAL GOODBYES

WE WERE HOME, and thoughts of what Carl had told me were at the forefront of my mind. I wanted to scream out and to tell Dad what had gone on, but I couldn't – I knew from telling him about Thomas that he would be ashamed of me and would probably have me sent away to prison. The dread of the whole family knowing – like they knew about Thomas – and looking down on me like I was an outcast was just too much. I couldn't bear that again for a second time around so I decided to keep it a secret, sparing my family any shame I would bring upon them.

Keeping this secret inside me turned me into a

rebel. I started to skip school to go and hang out with my friends at their houses, though of course each time I got caught either by my friends' parents or by the school. I wasn't very good at it; I was only ever good at getting into trouble with men.

It appeared that all the men in my life had become a disappointment to me; I was either ugly enough to be called 'four eyes', beautiful, or simply not listened to. I began to distrust everyone and took up smoking to supress my feelings; when I was smoking, it was impossible to feel anything. I had become accustomed to making sure I didn't break the rules or disobey. I was not loved, and I had no sympathy or kindness in my life – just existence. They would dole out the food, drink, and offer me shelter: 'keep my rules and I will not deprive you of your necessities'. That was it.

I didn't care about my behaviour as I lied to Angela, telling her I was staying at a friend's house when instead I would get on the train to go into London, hitting the clubs in Hammersmith and drinking. By now I had just turned sixteen and was able to get away with entering clubs so I could dance the night away. My dad was distancing himself from me, which didn't come as a shock as he hardly spent any time with me and Sarah anyway, and Angela cared more for her son than she did us, with his fancy private schooling and being able to sit in the family room with Dad and Angela to watch movies of an evening. I felt like a burden on everyone and so I began to distance myself too. All I ever wanted was to grow up, have a husband, and have lots of children, so I could treat them the complete opposite to how I was treated.

The time had come for me to do my exams, but I felt that hopeless with life itself that I didn't attend. What was the point, I kept saying to myself, until one afternoon when Sarah took me aside and told me to stop.

"Kelly," she said, "what are you doing? I know we don't like Angela, and Dad's no use 'cause he does everything she tells him to do, but one day we'll be free of them both. We've been through so much… do you want to ruin it now?"

I listened intently and knew that she was right, so I began to fill out college applications without any exam results to show for my talent, picking performing arts.

To my surprise I was accepted into college, and even found myself a part-time job in a theatre. I continued to smoke, but I was finally heading in the right track. I began to enjoy college and making new friends, all these experiences taking my mind off the other things in my life. I began to think about Mum, Thomas, and Carl less and less.

I served at the bistro in the theatre as I wasn't

old enough to be behind the bar, serving drinks. The bistro served all sorts of food – from jacket potatoes to steaks – and I would often start my shift at six in the evening, straight after college, and work till about nine. I started to finally enjoy my life and could see myself actually going somewhere.

Then, during one of my night shifts, I was approached by this slightly older gentleman called Michael, and we talked for what seemed like hours at the bar area. His hair short and light brown like crumpled leaves of Autumn. His eyes striking blue, full of life yet so uncertain. He was attractive I knew that. His lips swaying like the breeze as he spoke caring and fetching words. A gentle flush had arisen in his cheeks making him look vulnerable, had I wooed this man? I was in awe of his charm that was alluring and attractive at the same time. He made me laugh and told me a little about his life. He oversaw the lighting for the stage, making sure it was positioned correctly and turned on at the right times for each production.

With each shift I did at the theatre I found that I couldn't wait to see him. He was twenty-seven years old and he seemed so caring, always being interested in anything I had to say. Then, one day when I arrived for work, he asked me out on a date.

"Would you like to come for a drink after work tonight?" he asked shyly.

"Yes," I replied, all excited as I had never been asked out on a date before. I was sixteen and impressionable, yet very mature for my age as my life experience had given me some knowledge and skills.

He took me to a nearby pub, where everyone behind the bar seemed to know him; they all said hello to him, and also said how lovely it was to see him, which got me thinking this was a good thing.

We sat in a corner of the pub to talk further, and he went on to tell me that he'd recently come out of a long-term relationship and that she'd broken his heart. The way he spoke was extremely endearing; even though she'd broken his heart he found it very difficult to say any bad words about her. I, on the other hand, didn't see fit to discuss my life so much. The evening was full of laughter – something I felt I needed in my life right then.

That night I went home happy, twirling around my bedroom as I got undressed for bed. I hadn't felt like this since seeing Thomas, and it felt so good that someone had finally shown an interest in me. I laid my head on my pillow, dreaming of what might be and hoping he felt the same way.

I loved work and found myself racing to get there, even turning up early on occasion, and it was soon announced that Michael and I were dating – though my dad and Angela had no idea. I didn't feel it was right to let them know about anything that was going on in my personal life.

One night after a drink in the bar, Michael asked if I wanted to go to his place, and I agreed. I was excited to see how he lived, but most of all I was excited to get him alone.

He escorted me up the stairs that were situated at the back of some shops, as he lived in a flat above them. As we walked past another flat, one of his neighbours, Caroline, came out to empty some rubbish into the bins. "Hello Michael!" she called out. This was an even better sign, I thought: even his neighbours liked him and knew who he was.

As I entered his flat it seemed to be nice and light. The walls were plain, cream in colour with scarcely a picture anywhere. The bathroom was to the right and the living room and kitchen were open, with only a counter that separated the two rooms.

Michael seemed very modest as I approached him and tried to place a tender kiss upon his lips. To my surprise he pulled back and chuckled slightly, saying that I'd startled him.

This was new to me; I hadn't known a man to ever pull away from a kiss.

He offered me coffee, to which I responded yes, and then he apologised for the miscommunication, saying that he wanted to take things slowly considering he'd only recently split up with his girlfriend. I agreed, thinking how modest he was, and that he was a true gentleman. This must mean he really respected me, I thought, and didn't want to take anything for granted.

That evening we sat watching television, and I placed my head upon his chest as I relaxed. He didn't mind me doing it at all. He felt like my protector, and with him being older it reminded me of Dad all those years ago, when we lived in Germany and when I was able to rest upon his chest, feeling safe and secure.

I must have fallen asleep as when I awoke my head was on a pillow with a light blanket placed over me. It was dawn and I knew I would have to make my way home and explain where I'd been, yet I didn't want to go. I wanted to stay with this man forever and have him protect me and look after me, so I asked him whether I could stay. To my astonishment he said yes.

And so, there I was planning how I was going to tell Sarah, pack my things, and leave home. I was coming alive. I was feeling things I had only felt once before with Thomas – a strange aching and longing for this man. The throbbing, pulsating excitement ripped through me, knowing that a man was there for me. I wanted him to complete me, to give me a safe place to live and to love.

I made my way home in readiness to pack my belongings.

"Where are you going, Kelly?" Sarah asked, in a sad voice.

"I'm going to live with Michael, Sarah – I can't bear to be here any longer."

There was silence for a moment and then, in a quiet voice, she begged, "Please don't leave me here!"

I couldn't take her with me; I had only just turned sixteen and Sarah was too young to be parted from Dad. Gently, I caught her hands and pulled her to me. "In a couple of years, when you're old enough, you can come and live with me, I promise," I told her.

She bowed her head while I continued to pack.

A few minutes later, I almost chocked, drawing my breath, at my father stood in the room. Just like a thief, I had hoped to steal away with no one noticing, but there he stood: Dad.

When he spoke, his voice was cold. "Where are you going?"

My sudden escape had taken a turn for the worse, but I was determined not to be defeated. Turning my back on him to grab my bags, I replied, "I'm moving out!"

I was saying goodbye to the past and hello to the future – a bright future, for once in my life. So, I calmly made my way outside, a small smile piercing my lips, a smile I had long forgotten. I stood there for a moment, staring at the blue sky and taking in the cool air, ready for pastures new.

"Just remember: you've made your bed, now you can lie in it." Dad's words cut through me like a knife, swiftly removing my smile, and I jumped at the door slamming behind me.

Forbidding my tears to fall, I took a deep breath and continued on with my journey.

Enough was enough for now.

EPILOGUE

I stand in my new home, ready to put the past behind me, my past story feeling like it was never-ending. I survived, and I felt so blessed to have a sister by my side. She gave me strength and encouragement when I needed it the most. Considering my turbulent beginnings, I was lucky to have been rescued.

Being lucky also meant that I got to go on in life, to have a family of my own. To teach them right from wrong and to experience my childhood over again through my children. I have learnt to appreciate the finer things in life and to strive to be a better person – not only for myself but for my children too. I have learnt to forgive and forget, until very recent events brought me to write this book.

Despite going on to have wonderful children, my life has been an uphill struggle, and yet I've survived. I have triumphed through the good and the bad and have met so many people along the way. I am now a nurse and have achieved what I once thought was impossible, my goals and aspirations. I want to give back to others and share my compassion and love.

My past experience has driven me to write this first book, and I hope that I'll go on to write my second book, A Pawn in His Game. *I have come to realise that only you can make the impossible happen and only you can change your future from your past – no matter what your past was.*

Finally, I am free.

Finally, I am truly happy.

Printed in Poland
by Amazon Fulfillment
Poland Sp. z o.o., Wrocław

54969691R00141